MY HUGUENOT HERITAGE

Cover: *A Huguenot, on St Bartholomew's Day, Refusing to Shield Himself from Danger by Wearing the Roman Catholic Badge,* by John Everett Millais, 1851–2

MY
HUGUENOT
HERITAGE

A History of Persecution and Survival

ANTHEA RAMSAY

Fellow of the Huguenot Society of Great Britain and Ireland

Matador
Unit E2 Airfield Business Park,
Harrison Road, Market Harborough,
Leicestershire. LE16 7UL
Tel: 0116 2792299
Email: books@troubador.co.uk
Web: www.troubador.co.uk/matador
Twitter: @matadorbooks

ISBN 978 1800463 042

British Library Cataloguing in Publication Data.
A catalogue record for this book is available from the British Library.

Typeset in 12pt Adobe Caslon Pro by Troubador Publishing Ltd, Leicester, UK

Matador is an imprint of Troubador Publishing Ltd

For my eight grandchildren

A STORY BASED ON FACT

Using the wealth of written material that has survived in the form of family memoirs, documents, early biographies, and history books, I have tried to be as factual as is possible when writing about people and events from so long ago.

CONTENTS

PART TWO ENGLAND 1685 –1872

PART THREE AUSTRALIA 1848

Sixteenth-Century Map of France

LE PLASTRIER FAMILY TREE
1395 - 1918

Jean and Rachel (née Du Garde) and most of their children escaped to England after the Revocation of the Edict of Nantes in 1685. One of their sons Robert went back to France in 1709 with his third wife Marie (née Le Blanc) and their four children. They all died there, apart from my ancestor Isaac who returned to carry on the Le Plastrier name in England.

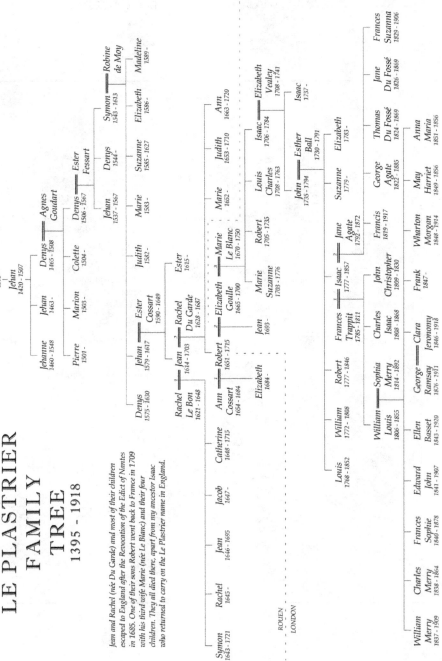

KINGS OF FRANCE FROM 1364

House of Valois 1328–1589
House of Lancaster 1422–1453
House of Bourbon 1589–1792

MONARCH	REIGNED FROM	DIED
Charles V	8 April 1364	16 September 1380
Charles VI	16 September 1380	21 October 1422
Henry VI*	21 October 1422 (disputed)	19 October 1453
Charles VII	21 October 1422	22 July 1461
Louis XI	22 July 1461	30 August 1483
Charles VIII	30 August1483	7 April 1498
Louis XII	7 April 1498	1 January 1515
François I	1 January 1515	31 March 1547
Henri II	31 March 1547	10 July 1559
François II	10 July 1559	5 December 1560
Charles IX	5 December 1560	30 May 1574
Henri III	30 May 1574	2 August 1589
Henri IV	2 August 1589	14 May 1610
Louis XIII	14 May 1610	14 May 1643
Louis XIV	14 May 1643	1 September 1715

* Henry VI of the House of Lancaster, grandson of Charles VI of France, by right of his father Henry V of England, who by the Treaty of Troyes became heir and regent of France.

PRINCIPAL CHARACTERS

HOUSE OF VALOIS 1328 –1589 (Founded in 1284)

Charles VI, son of Charles V and Jeanne de Bourbon. Married to Isabeau of Bavaria

Charles VII, son of Charles VI and Isabeau of Bavaria. Married to Marie d'Anjou

François I, son of Charles, Compte d'Angoulême, and Louise de Savoie. Succeeded his cousin and father-in-law Louis XII, who died without an heir. Married to Claude, Duchess of Brittany, and after her death to Eleanor of Castile

Marguerite d'Angoulême, sister of François I. Married to Henri d'Albret, King of Navarre. A Protestant sympathiser

Dauphin François, Duke of Brittany, eldest son of François I and Claude, Duchess of Brittany. Predeceased his younger brother Henri d'Orleans

Henri II, 2nd son of François I and Claude, Duchess of Brittany. Married to Catherine de Médicis, daughter of Lorenzo II de' Medici and Madeleine de La Tour d'Auvergne

François II, eldest son of Henri II and Catherine de Médicis. Married to Mary, Queen of Scots

Charles IX, 2nd son of Henri II and Catherine de Médicis. Married to Elisabeth of Austria

Henri III, Duc d'Anjou, 3rd son of Henri II and Catherine de Médicis. Married to Louise de Lorraine-Vaudémont. Henri died without an heir

François, Duc d'Alençon [known as 'Monsieur'] later Duc d'Anjou, youngest son of Henri II and Catherine de Médicis. Predeceased Henri III, thereby ending the rule of the House of Valois

Elisabeth de Valois, daughter of Henri II and Catherine de Médicis. Married to Philip II of Spain

Claude de Valois, daughter of Henri II and Catherine de Médicis. Married to Charles III, Duc de Lorraine

Marguerite de Valois, daughter of Henri II and Catherine de Médicis. Married to Henri de Bourbon, King of Navarre, later King Henri IV, 1st Bourbon king of France

HOUSE OF BOURBON 1272–1830

Antoine de Bourbon, King of Navarre, 1st prince of the blood. Married to Jeanne d'Albret, Queen of Navarre, daughter of Marguerite d'Angoulême and Henri d'Albret, King of Navarre. A Huguenot

Louis de Bourbon, Prince de Condé, 2nd prince of the blood, brother of Antoine de Bourbon, King of Navarre. A prominent Huguenot leader

Charles, Cardinal de Bourbon, 3rd prince of the blood, brother of Antoine de Bourbon, and Louis, Prince de Condé. Persuaded by the Guises and King Philip II of Spain to become the pretender, Charles X to keep the Protestant Henri de Bourbon off the throne

Henri de Bourbon, son of Antoine de Bourbon and Jeanne d'Albret, King and Queen of Navarre. Became king of Navarre on the death of his mother. Inherited the throne of France from Henri III in 1589 and became Henri IV, the first Protestant Bourbon king. Converted to Catholicism, and was crowned in 1594. 1st wife: Marguerite de Valois, daughter of Henri II and Catherine de Médicis, 2nd wife Marie de' Medici. He was responsible for the Edict of Nantes, signed in April 1598, granting Huguenots substantial rights

Louis XIII son of Henri IV and Marie de' Medici. Married to Anne of Austria

Louis XIV, son of King Louis XIII and Anne of Austria. He was responsible for the Revocation of the Edict of Nantes in 1685

HOUSE OF GUISE 1496–1675

Claude, 1st Duc de Guise, son of René, Duc de Lorraine

François, 2nd Duc de Guise, eldest son of Claude, 1st Duc de Guise. Married to Anna d'Este

Charles, Cardinal de Lorraine, 2nd son of Claude, 1st Duc de Guise

Claude, Duc d'Aumale, 5th son of Claude, 1st Duc de Guise

Marie de Guise, daughter of Claude, 1st Duc de Guise. Married to James V of Scotland

Mary, Queen of Scots, daughter of Marie de Guise and James V of Scotland. Married to François II

Henri Duc de Guise, son of François, 2nd Duc de Guise and Anna d'Este. Murdered by Henri III

Louis, Cardinal de Guise, brother of Henri, Duc de Guise. Murdered by Henri III

HOUSE OF BURGUNDY 1032–1361

Philip the Bold, Duc de Burgundy, founder of the Burgundian branch of the House of Valois

John the Fearless, Duc de Burgundy, son of Philip the Bold

Philip the Good, Duc de Burgundy, son of John the Fearless

Charles the Bold, last Duc de Burgundy, son of Philip the Good

HOUSE OF MONTMORENCY

Anne de Montmorency – Anne is pronounced Annay – Great Constable of France, son of William de Montmorency and Anne St Pol. Married to Madeleine de Savoie

François de Montmorency, eldest son of Anne de Montmorency

Married to Diane de France, illegitimate daughter of Henri II, later legitimised

Henri Damville de Montmorency, 2nd son of Anne de Montmorency

Charles de Montmorency, 3rd son of Anne de Montmorency

Gabriel de Montmorency, 4th son of Anne de Montmorency

Gaspard de Coligny, Admiral of France, nephew of Anne de Montmorency. Undisputed leader of the Huguenots

Ôdet de Coligny, Cardinal de Châtillon, elder brother of Gaspard de Coligny. A leading Huguenot

François d'Andelot de Coligny, youngest brother of Gaspard de Coligny. A leading Huguenot

OTHER

John Calvin, French theologian, pastor and father of Calvinism and the Protestant Church

Diane de Poitiers, Duchesse de Valentinois, declared mistress of Henri II

Michel de l'Hôpital, chancellor to Catherine de Médicis. A moderate

Michel de Nostradamus, seer to Catherine de Médicis

Niccolò Machiavelli author of *The Prince*, dedicated to Lorenzo de' Medici, Duke of Urbino. Catherine followed many of his harsh principles

François-Michel le Tellier, Marquis de Louvois, referred to as 'Louvois'. French Secretary of State for War, and enemy of the Huguenots. Responsible for organising the billeting of dragoons in the homes of Huguenots in various cities including Poitou and Rouen

René de Marillac, an intendant responsible for carrying out the billeting of dragoons in the homes of Huguenots to coerce them to convert to Catholicism

MAIN PEACE EDICTS

Edict of January, signed by Catherine de Médicis as regent for Charles IX in 1562. This granted a small measure of liberty for Huguenots to practise their faith outside city walls and town centres

Edict of Pacification, or Edict of Amboise, signed by Catherine de Médicis as regent for Charles IX on 19 March 1563. Similar to the Edict of January, but officially ended the first phase of the Wars of Religion

Peace of Saint-Germain-en-Laye, signed by Charles IX on 5 August 1570. Negotiated by Jeanne d'Albret, Queen of Navarre. Ended the third War of Religion

Peace of Monsieur or Edict of Beaulieu, signed by Henri III, against his will, on 6 May 1576 granting land and titles to Huguenot nobles

Edict of Nantes, signed on 13 April 1598 by Henri IV, which granted large measures of liberty to the Huguenots

INTRODUCTION

I felt compelled to dig further into my origins when I inherited family papers and books, narrating the lives of my French ancestors from the fourteenth to the nineteenth century. I discovered that we are descended from Huguenots who, after suffering relentless persecution, were forced to flee to England and Holland in 1685. The family name was Le Plastrier, and they lived in Rouen.

I knew very little about the Huguenots, but soon learnt that they were Catholics who converted to Protestantism in the sixteenth century. For many years France had held a Catholic monarchy and kings viewed their authority as a divine right – *une foi, une loi, un roi* – one faith, one law, one king. This meant that most citizens were Catholic until around 1530 when many began to follow the Protestant teachings of Jehan Cauvin – better known as John Calvin. To begin with the converts were called Calvinists but later became known as Huguenots. It is not known how the name came about, and there are many theories, none of which have been validated. Some say that it began as an insult, but Huguenot descendants prefer to think of the name as a badge of honour symbolising courage and endurance through centuries of oppression, inhumanity, and massacres.

Huguenots never exceeded Catholics by more than ten percent of the population, yet, despite being thought of as heretics by many, their influence was immense.

This was at a time when the impact of the Protestant Reformation was being felt throughout Europe; the other great protagonist being a German, Martin Luther. His followers were henceforth known as Lutherans. The word 'Protestantism' originated from the Protest Movement against the excesses of the Catholic Church. The 'New Religion' was also becoming popular in England; Henry VIII having dispensed with the pope and the Catholic Church and changed the religion of England to Protestantism in 1534 in order to marry Anne Boleyn. John Knox later embraced the Reformation and established the Presbyterian Church of Scotland.

The French nobility were among the first to leave the Catholic Church to follow Calvin, since the idea of having a church led by him and not Rome greatly appealed to them. This was a huge threat to the king, as the nobility were closely entwined with the monarchy. Later, people from across the social scale and occupational divide began to convert, many holding important positions in commerce and industry. Huguenots, as well as posing a threat to the monarchy, were considered heretics by the pope and *parlement* – parliament. In these pages the word usually refers to the main anti-Protestant body of Paris, although there were other more minor provincial *parlements*. In sixteenth-century France they wielded enormous power as they were not just legislative bodies, but provincial high courts controlled by red-robed judges and nobles. No law or edict issued by the crown was made official until passed by them. They usually delayed accepting an edict in favour of the Protestants for as long as possible, especially in Paris.

Over the years the loyal and steadfast Huguenots were burned, beheaded, or tied up in sacks and thrown into rivers to drown on the orders of despotic kings or regents, but their unshakeable and heroic faith helped them to sustain unspeakable cruelty. Such barbaric acts eventually forced them to rebel, thereby igniting the Wars of Religion which lasted from 1562 to 1598. These wars were broken by spells of armed truce and peace agreements, mainly involving a dynastic power struggle between the wealthy, ambitious Catholic House of Guise and the – *princes du sang* – princes of the blood from the aristocratic Protestant House of Condé, a branch of the House of Bourbon, each as intransigent as the other.

François II, Charles IX, and Henri III were sons of Catherine de Médicis and Henri II, and during their reigns Huguenots were persistently persecuted. Peace prevailed for a time when the Protestant Henri de Bourbon inherited the throne in 1589 after the death of his Valois cousin Henri III and became Henri IV, the first Bourbon king. He fought against the Catholics in the Wars of Religion but was forced to convert to Catholicism in order to be crowned. At heart he remained sympathetic to the Huguenots and in April 1598 he signed the Edict of Nantes, which for the first time gave them widespread religious liberties and a few years of relative peace. They became increasingly successful, which antagonised the pope, the clergy, and the more radical Catholics, instigating more unrest.

Shockingly, Louis XIV revoked the edict in October 1685 which meant that Huguenots had no rights at all, and no protection from their church. If they refused to convert, or attempted to leave, it was considered heresy. As many as twenty-five *dragonnades* – dragoons – were billeted in a single home and told to 'do as they wished'[1] with the women and children in order to coerce the family into signing the abjuration papers.

Huguenots had to decide whether to stay true to their faith, defy the law and flee, or accept the benefits offered to them by the king and revert to Catholicism. If they decided to leave this usually meant surrendering wealth for poverty and tearing the family apart. Faced with this decision many recanted while others decided to save their souls and escape. Some left young children and elderly parents behind to be cared for by Catholic friends. They often never saw them again.

After having been persecuted by cruel *dragonnades*, the more ardent and sincere Huguenots such as my ancestors chose to risk their lives and flee. They agreed to convert with their lips, but not with their hearts, and to sign the abjuration papers, while secretly planning their dangerous escape to a country where they could practise their faith in peace.

It is estimated that more than two hundred thousand Huguenots chose exile rather than apostasy, and, using dangerous and innovative subterfuges, fled to countries where there was greater tolerance and a large Protestant movement existed, such as the Netherlands, parts of Germany, Switzerland, and Scandinavia. In excess of forty thousand escaped to England and the Channel Islands. Later, many moved much further afield. The Dutch East India Company sent hundreds of Huguenots to the Cape of Good Hope in South Africa to help develop the vineyards. They soon assimilated with the Dutch colonialists who shared religious similarities. Many intermarried, and some were given farms, which are still owned by their descendants.

France suffered hugely after the flight of the Huguenots, as it was deprived of thousands of its most industrious and successful citizens. Prosperous families not only carried away money and gold, but also valuable connections with foreign markets. Others took with them their expertise in the arts and sciences. They were all welcomed with open arms by their adoptive countries, and many remained happily in the countries that had given them sanctuary in their time of need.

I have tried to write the story of the trials and tribulations endured by my ancestors, and Huguenots as a whole, during the traumatic years in France as accurately and sensitively as possible. I hope you will find their story as interesting and moving as I do.

The Huguenot Monument in
Franschhoek, Western Cape South Africa

PROLOGUE

◇━◧━◇━━◇━━◧━◇

Delving Into The Past

It is thanks to my great-great-great-grandfather Isaac Le Plastrier and his brother Louis that we have so much first-hand information illustrating what life was like for my ancestors, and Huguenots in general, during the years of persecution and injustice. Nearly one hundred and thirty years after their progenitor Jean fled France to start a new life in England, the brothers travelled from Dover to the courts of Rouen. Their aim was to reclaim three valuable properties that had been sequestrated when Jean and his family escaped. To prove that they were entitled to ownership, it was necessary for their legal team to dig deep into the past for documents and Last Wills and Testaments.

Unfortunately, they lost the case, but undaunted the brothers returned four years later to appeal the decision. They lost the appeal, as well as the family inheritance. However, they left invaluable previously unknown facts, chronicling the travails of the Le Plastriers from the fourteenth century. These documents have given us a wonderful insight into the characters and lives of our ancestors, and have been reverently preserved and passed down the family through the years. Now future generations can enjoy our fascinating heritage.

Like most Huguenots the Le Plastriers were benevolent, law-abiding and hard-working people who were loyal to their family, their faith, and their king. They were successful businessmen rather than artisans. By the sixteenth century many had become merchants and goldsmiths owning land on the outskirts of Rouen, as well as some large properties in the centre of the city.

In September 2005, armed with the family tree and all the papers and documents accumulated over the years, I decided to travel to Rouen and continue the search for more information about my ancestors. The city straddles both sides of the River Seine and was one of the largest and most prosperous of medieval Europe. It is now the capital of Normandy and is renowned for the magnificent Notre-Dame Cathedral, immortalised by Monet in several of his paintings. It is also famous for being the place where Joan of Arc was tried and burned at the stake.

Regrettably, many of the beautiful old buildings in the town have been razed, but the narrow streets and ancient buildings in the area surrounding Notre-Dame and the famous rue du Gros Horloge – the Street of the Great Clock – where many Le Plastriers resided remain intact. It is known by this name due to its beautiful, ornate astronomical clock which sits above a low Renaissance arch spanning the entire street. Jourdain del Leche began constructing the clock in 1389 but it was a huge project, and he did not have the expertise or the time to finish the task. It was later completed by Jean de Felain, who became the first person to hold the position of Governor of the Clock. It was installed in its present location in 1529.

The façade shows a globe consisting of twenty-four sun rays on a blue background, with the phases of the moon on the oculus of the upper part. Weekdays are shown in an opening at the base of the dial, which is surrounded by allegorical figures for each day of the week, including paintings of sheep depicting the importance of the historic wool trade. This huge, imposing clock is featured in a painting by Joseph Mallord William Turner – *The Gros Horloge at Rouen, Normandy* c. 1832.

Several street names remain today as they were all those years ago, which enabled me to easily pinpoint where many of my ancestors' homes once stood. I was enthralled to stumble upon 23 rue du Gros Horloge – the only house once owned and lived in by them which still remains. It is a beautiful four-storey, seventeenth-century, half-timbered building richly decorated with wood corbelling. The house sits proudly among other similar four and five storey properties, situated between the towering Notre-Dame and the famous clock in what is now the main tourist area. I was delighted to find that it had been sympathetically renovated on the outside with an antique shop on the ground floor. The remaining floors seemed empty and dark and I felt that a great sense of despair and foreboding clung to the walls, but perhaps that was just my imagination.

I wondered if my ancestors had been subjected to having *dragonnades* forced upon them in this particular house. This we will never know as the gloomy windows held their secret well. The owner of the antique shop showed me the small cellar where the family once stored their gold; the entrance of which is now covered with reinforced glass. This was one of the properties seized when my ancestors were forced to flee. It was also one of the houses Isaac and Louis attempted to reclaim. I tried in vain to find the other two properties, but they had obviously been demolished in the intervening years.

The charming hotel in which I stayed was ideally situated in a rambling old house in rue des Carmes, close to Notre-Dame. After some research I discovered that this was the very road, and possibly the same house, in which my ancestor Marie Le Blanc, later married to Robert Le Plastrier, once lived with her family. They fled to Amsterdam after they had endured the indignity and brutality of having *dragonnades* billeted in their home.

As I sat at a pavement café on the rue du Gros Horloge, gazing in awe at the magnificent clock, my thoughts were caught in the past. I imagined my ancestors walking swiftly through the dark, dangerous, narrow arches and alleyways, their long black cloaks swaying as they made their way to worship at the Quevilly Temple – the famous Huguenot church.

I pondered upon the anguish Huguenots must have suffered during the massacres, and later when threatened with having ruthless soldiers billeted in their beautiful homes, knowing that they had been told to do as they wished with the women and children. Walking in my ancestors' footsteps along the same, sombre, cobbled streets close to the cathedral, I was aware that Symon Le Plastrier, a goldsmith and merchant, had lived in a property named Maison Amail which once stood on the corner of rue Grand-Pont and Place de la Cathédrale. Horrifically, he and his wife and daughter were murdered at sea while attempting to escape, but more of that in a later chapter.

How privileged I was to have so much information about my ancestors, but I was impatient to unlock more secrets. I also hoped to learn more about how they had endured those terrible times, and to discover how they had managed to effect their escape. However, further research was to prove difficult. I soon discovered that this was a subject local people were reluctant to discuss. It was a period in history of which France was not proud. Very few records were kept, as Protestants in those perilous times were often forbidden to record marriages, christenings, or burials. Consequently, these ceremonies were carried out covertly, many graves forever hidden, and important dates never officially recorded.

It was thrilling to discover the reclamation yard at the Museum of Antiquities where ancient beams, half eaten away by the passage of time, and stoneware saved from demolished properties had all been lovingly preserved. I stumbled across several old signs, which were the same as those that are known to have hung on the exterior of some of my ancestors' homes. Humbled, I stood amidst this tragic history, aware that most of these salvaged articles were originally from abandoned Huguenot properties.

The curator of the museum was extremely helpful and, despite my inadequate French, seemed very interested in my connection to the

Calvinists, which is how the local people still refer to the Huguenots. He even produced a very dirty copper plaque, known as a Table of Copper, dating back to 1562 when Rouen was besieged and captured by the Royalists, with the names and marks of the three hundred goldsmiths who were registered, including some Le Plastriers. I was delighted to find this treasure, especially when the curator promised to clean it and send me a photograph. He kept his word and the package arrived shortly after my return to England.

PART ONE

France 1395–1685

CHAPTER ONE

Origins Of The Le Plastrier Family

The Huguenots were, with rare exceptions, the most decorous, the most upright, the most intelligent and the most frugal citizens.[1]

H. M. Baird

The Le Plastriers are descended from Norsemen, who were descended from marauding warrior Vikings from Scandinavia. From the eighth century they plundered and raided continental coastlines, terrorising the inhabitants. In 911 Rouen was captured during the Siege of Chartres by a Viking chief named Rollo. In the hope that he would cease attacking their ports the king, Charles the Simple, ceded him land in northern France. Rollo, who it is said had a very long nose and was so tall that when riding his legs almost touched the ground, became the first ruler of what we now call Normandy.

For a further century the descendants of Rollo were known

as pirates or sea wolves. Eventually many intermarried with the French, lost their identity and culture, abandoned paganism, and became Christians. Famous for their martial spirit they successfully invaded southern Italy and Sicily, and in 1066 William, Duke of Normandy – William the Conqueror – a descendant of Rollo, famously attacked and defeated the English at the Battle of Hastings. He was assisted by some of my ancestors from the Le Blanc side of my family.

The first known Le Plastriers are Giriaume and Betrant, who are mentioned in the Paris census of 1292, after which the trail goes cold until the fourteenth century. Although Giriaume and Betrant lived in Rouen, they were recorded in this census as Rouen was then the port of Paris. Arthur Edwin Le Plastrier surmises in his book *A Brief History of the Le Plastrier Family*, written in 1944, that the name Le Plastrier may have been derived from the old French word *plastron*, which meant breastplate. However, Denis Le Plastrier Webb suggests in his later book *The Le Plastrier and Allied Families*, written in 1984, that the name originated from the word *plastrier*, which meant plasterer – now written *plâtrier* in modern dictionaries. Surnames usually originated from an individual's occupation, their father's first name, their appearance, or some particular trait or peculiarity that they may have possessed. Le Plastrier remained an unusual name as there were not many skilled plasterers, unlike, for instance, the many bakers with the name Le Boulanger, or ironworkers with the name Lefèvre.

Denis Le Plastrier Webb writes that he is in possession of a letter from the archivist of the Department of the Seine-Maritime in Rouen, referring to a Le Plastrier in their records, which read:

> *Lorens Hèrouf, autrement dit Le Plastrier, et Jeanne sa femme, prennant en fief et perpetual heritage de Gautier de la Mare et de Tiphaigne, sa femme, un tenement avec les edifices dessus mis paroisse St Martin Jouxte Le Pont [Rouen].*[2]

Roughly translated, this means: Lorens Hèrouf, otherwise known as The Plasterer, and Jeanne his wife, took as his stronghold and everlasting heritage from Gautier de la Mare and Tiphaigne, his wife, a holding with nicely turned-out buildings in the parish of St Martin Jouxte le Pont [Rouen]. As Lorens was nicknamed 'Le Plastrier' this indicates that he was also my progenitor and that this is very likely the start of the family name. Plasterers decorated the ceilings of palaces and châteaux with ornate gilding, and their special techniques may have been one of the reasons why some of them became goldsmiths. Research shows that there was only one family of Le Plastriers in the fourteenth century, but we will never know how Lorens and Jeanne were related to Giriaume and Betrant.

Prior to the sixteenth century the Le Plastriers were Catholic and some remained true to their beliefs, but my ancestors eventually joined the Calvinist movement and became staunch Protestants. Much later some became pastors of the famous Quevilly Temple in Rouen, where they congregated to pray and seek sanctuary during dangerous times. Like all scripture-loving Huguenots they preferred to choose biblical forenames for their children, which was just as well as the names of saints were normally chosen by Catholics. Certain patron saints' names were traditionally handed down from generation to generation amongst old French families.

My ancestors eventually became merchants and goldsmiths, but after fleeing France they made clocks, chronometers, and watches in London and Kent. This venture turned into a successful business passed down from father to son. Today any timepiece created by a Le Plastrier is a rare and expensive find.

In an era where pedigree and social status were paramount the family held a tradition of marrying the sons and daughters of other merchants such as the Le Blancs, Cossarts, Du Gardes, and Du Ponts. They were also inclined to marry first and second cousins, so from that perspective it was a good thing that they were eventually forced to flee and spread their wings. They were among the first to escape after Louis XIV revoked the Edict of Nantes, when it was most dangerous.

One of the most authoritative sources of information on Huguenots is a book by Colonel H. A. Du Pont. It consists of two volumes entitled *The Early Generations of the Du Pont and Allied Families* and can be found in the Huguenot Library in London. Details regarding the Le Plastriers are contained in the seventeenth and eighteenth chapters. The early Du Ponts lived in Rouen and were closely aligned to my ancestors through marriage. Not all converted and many remained in France. They are now scattered all over the world. Some emigrated to America, where they founded the huge organisation of Du Pont de Nemours, Inc. Coincidentally, my son, Grant, is married to Emilie, whose mother was born a Du Pont – now spelt Dupont.

CHAPTER TWO

⟨⟩━━◆━━⟨⟩━━━━━━━⟨⟩━━◆━━⟨⟩

The Siege Of Rouen

*France was everywhere the scene of such acts as belong
exclusively to the reign of war.*[1]

H. M. Baird

D enys Le Plastrier was born in 1395 and lived with his
family in the parish of Saint-Éloi on the outskirts of
the city. He was a political figure and therefore held
a responsible position. The name of his wife is unknown, but
fortunately Denys survived Henry V of England's devastating
siege and fathered a son, Jehan, or there would be no story for me
to write about.

During Denys's lifetime Charles VI of the House of Valois was
king. He inherited the throne at the age of eleven after the death
of his father, Charles V, in 1380 in the midst of the Hundred Years'
War against England. As he was not permitted to rule until he
was fifteen his two conniving, grasping uncles the Duc de Berry
and the Duc de Burgundy – known as Philip the Bold – were
regents. They were unpopular and incompetent dictators who

clung avariciously to their power until the king was twenty-one.

The financial reserves, which had been so diligently built up by his father, were plundered by the uncles causing uprisings and raised taxes. Charles V's sobriquet was *Charles le Sage*, as he was thought of as a wise but stern king with shrewd and prudent advisors called the *Marmousets* – Little Monkeys. By the end of his life, he had restored the esteem of the House of Valois and reconquered almost all of the territories which had been surrendered to the English in 1360. He was also the first French king to hold the title of dauphin until his coronation. All heirs to the throne subsequently bore this title. Eventually, an older and wiser Charles VI dismissed his interfering uncles and reinstated his father's *Marmousets*, and political and economic conditions improved for a time. But towards the end of his mainly disastrous reign most of the cities and towns, which had been reclaimed by his father, had again been seized by the English.

Charles VI reigned for forty-two years and at the start of his sovereignty was known as *le Bien-Aimé* – the Beloved. He was married to the beautiful but formidable and promiscuous Isabeau of Bavaria. The marriage was not a happy one, although they both enjoyed spending money and attending debauched, risqué banquets and masked balls. Everything changed when he began hallucinating and behaving in a strange manner. On a blazing hot day in August 1392, while travelling through the forest near Le Mans with his army the king suddenly erupted into an unprovoked psychotic fit of violence, killing several knights and injuring his younger brother Louis d'Orléans. It is believed that his mental illness, which may have been passed on in different forms for several generations, was inherited from his mother, Jeanne de Bourbon.

This was the onset of his thirty-year struggle with prolonged periods of insanity. Charles now became known as *le Fou* – the Mad. He started having intermittent delusions, denying that he was king or that he had a wife and children, and believing that he was made of glass. He became violent, babbled incoherently, refused to bathe, smeared excrement all over himself, and made obscene gestures.

The king's illness gave his elderly uncle Philip the Bold a reason to banish his advisors and retake control of governing the kingdom. Meanwhile, the king's equally ambitious eighteen-year-old brother Louis, seeing his ascendancy in danger, speedily stepped into the fray.

A year after the incident at Le Mans, Isabeau organised a masked ball to celebrate the wedding of one of her ladies-in-waiting. It was held at the king's Paris residence and place of his birth, the *Hôtel* Saint-Pol. Louis, holding a lighted torch, decided to try and discover the identity of one of the lords who was among those masquerading as wild men dressed in costumes of linen cloth, which had been sewn onto their bodies and soaked in resinous wax. Unfortunately, he accidentally set one of them on fire. The fire soon spread throughout the room, burning four of the lords to death and badly injuring several knights who were trying to put the flames out. This tragedy has gone down in history as the *Bal des Ardents* – Ball of the Burning Men.

The king kept a mistress, Odette de Champdivers, with whom he had a daughter. Unlike Isabeau, Odette was able to pacify Charles when he was unwell, and he spent much of his time with her. In between periods of insanity he behaved normally, recognised his wife and children, and resumed governing the country. Louis and Philip were only too eager to hold the reins of power during the king's bouts of lunacy. This caused huge confusion as Charles was sometimes considered sane enough to rule, and his subjects still thought of him as their beloved sovereign. Every policy implemented by Philip or Louis had to be delivered in Charles's name, which deluded the populace into thinking that he was capable and well.

The king's madness was the undoing of France for many years to come. Although at times he seemed lucid, he was highly susceptible to intrigue and plots and therefore often unaware of what he was signing. Louis, taking advantage of his brother's unpredictable mental state, persuaded him to gift him two valuable properties knowing that Philip the Bold coveted them. Philip was so infuriated that he retaliated by raising an army and attempted to capture Paris. As Charles was confined with his mistress at the *Hôtel* Saint-Pol, Isabeau, who until then had kept out of political matters, was forced to mediate and cleverly managed to prevent civil war at the eleventh hour.

In a moment of sanity, the king saw his wife in a new light. He declared that if he was indisposed, Isabeau was sanctioned to manage internal affairs. She was quick to take advantage of her powerful new position and became greedy, covetous, and unpopular. No woman was permitted to make decisions on her own, so she manipulated her brother-in-law Louis, who was equally avaricious and promiscuous, to advise her. They caused great scandal, not only due to their dissipated morals and the rumour that Louis was her lover, but because they used every opportunity to line their pockets with public money. All this gossip suited Philip and his faction, the Burgundians, who were probably responsible for much of it in the first place. Louis and Isabeau's behaviour made them easy targets.

Charles played one against the other, with Philip having control one minute and Isabeau and Louis the next, causing more envy, suspicion, and intrigue. When Philip the Bold died his eldest son John the Fearless, now the Duc de Burgundy and equally ambitious, joined the quest for power. Matters culminated one night in November 1407. Louis was walking through a dark passage, after spending the evening with Isabeau, when a group of armed men leapt menacingly out of the shadows. Thinking that it was a random attack he shouted that he was Louis d'Orleans the king's brother. 'It is you we want,'[2] came the ominous reply, as they hacked Louis and his knights to death. John the Fearless later admitted to organising this heinous crime yet managed to avoid being censured for it until twelve years later, when the dauphin – the future Charles VII – avenged the murder of his uncle by arranging for John the Fearless to be slaughtered on the bridge of Montereau.

The assassination of Louis was the start of a bitter blood feud between the House of Burgundy, a secondary branch of the royal family, and the Armagnacs of the House of Orléans, a primary branch of the royal family who supported the king and the House of Valois.

Henry V of England, who thrived on warfare, took advantage of these factional disputes by occupying his time seizing towns in Normandy. After his astonishing victory against the far stronger French troops at the Battle of Agincourt, followed by the capture of Caen, full of confidence he set his sights on Rouen. He wanted the city because its strategic position made the capture crucial to his campaign. At the time Rouen was the most impregnable city Henry's army had yet faced, as the walls were protected by sixty towers, each containing three cannons.

At the onset of the siege John the Fearless, having occupied Paris, at first refused to help. He eventually dispatched four thousand men-at-arms, with Guy le Bouteiller as the overall commander, including one hundred crossbow men led by Alain Blanchard. The city itself had in the region of sixteen thousand civilians, along with men from other parts of Normandy who had fled when their own towns had been destroyed and were eager to fight the English. Nevertheless, they were dangerously under-armed. Although the city was already well fortified, the inhabitants decided to strengthen it further so that the enemy would be unable to enter.

They began their preparation for defence by destroying all the houses and buildings on the south side of the river to ensure that the adversary had no cover. With large stones and other materials now available, they repaired and strengthened the walls. Slings for hurling heavy darts and arrows were set up on the Port Martainville, and every boat on the river above or below the city was sunk. Taxes were raised and families were advised to stock up with food for the next ten months – rather optimistic as the province was in dire straits and there was a desperate shortage of food. Thus, they waited for the attack.

The siege began on 29 July 1418 when Henry set out with his army of over forty-five thousand men consisting of captains, barons, knights, cavalry, carpenters, and engineers. They set up four fortified camps and barricaded the River Seine with iron chains. The *Rouennais* woke one morning to find that they were surrounded; Henry having got his troops into position during the night. They were completely cut off from any hope or help. The city was so well protected that the strategy of the English was to surround the walls and starve out the defenders. They gradually began to cut Rouen off from the rest of the country, but the inhabitants continued to put up a brave fight and incredibly managed to keep the attackers at bay. Not surprisingly, starvation and disease soon took hold. In desperation, the *Rouennais* sent a messenger to Paris to seek additional help from Charles and John the Fearless. They warned them that if they were forced to surrender the king could count on them becoming bitter enemies, but, regardless of the threats and many promises, no assistance came. By December the situation was so critical that to remain alive people were forced to drink urine and foul ditch water, and to eat cats, dogs, and horses. When these delicacies were depleted, those who survived were driven to chewing scraps of clothing, or leather boiled in vinegar to soften it enough to swallow.

Denys was one of the men responsible for many of the difficult decisions that had to be made to save the lives of the remaining stalwarts, and to keep the soldiers with their crossbows strong enough to stand behind the thick walls surrounding the city. Eventually, they were compelled to turn out those who had sought sanctuary from ruined nearby towns. Starving men, women, and children staggered out of the gates and made their exhausted, hopeful way to the English lines. Predictably, no help was forthcoming and they had to survive as well as they could while living in the ditches and drains surrounding the walls. Without shelter, sleeping in their own excrement, ragged, defenceless, and feeding on grubs, roots, and rodents most of the refugees lost their lives. Many died from chance missiles fired by both sides or of starvation. An emaciated priest sporadically leant over the walls with a blessing, or to pull up a newborn child to baptise before lowering it down again to die. At one stage the starving citizens were so distraught that they thought of setting fire to the whole city or rushing out to the English to 'do or die'. Eventually, those who survived surrendered.

After the fall, the people were so disenchanted by the lack of help they had received from their king that they swore allegiance to Henry. Nearly six months later what remained of the French soldiers marched out. Alain Blanchard was immediately captured and beheaded in retaliation for all The English soldiers he had ordered to be executed. The bells rang out and cannons were fired in salute as Henry entered the city, but the few remaining inhabitants were so weak and hungry that they could hardly stand, much less welcome the English king.

Rouen became the principal base for Henry to continue launching his successful campaign. He soon occupied much of northern France, including Paris, but was determined to seize the rest of the country. After months of negotiations, he finally persuaded the unstable Charles to sign the Treaty of Troyes in May 1420, disinheriting the dauphin. Henry was appointed regent and his heirs were recognised as the legitimate successors to the French throne. As part of the agreement he married the king's youngest daughter, the beautiful Catherine de Valois, and took her to live in Windsor where in December of the following year he fathered the future king of England and France.

Henry's dream never materialised, as although he was younger than Charles he died before him on 31 August 1422, aged thirty-six, at Château de Vincennes. His demise was caused by the 'bloody flux' – dysentery – after being wounded while successfully capturing Meaux. He was carried through the streets of Rouen on his funeral bier, only fifty days before the French crown would have been his.

Catherine de Valois was left a young widow in a foreign land, lonely and vulnerable, living at Windsor Castle with her nine-month-old son. He was now Henry VI, head of the House of Lancaster, and became the disputed king of France upon the death of his grandfather, the mad Charles VI, less than two months later.

CHAPTER THREE

Jehan Le Plastrier, The Entrepreneur

Scarcely could the royal troops have been more actively employed in declared war.[1]

H. M. Baird

When Jehan Le Plastrier was born shortly after the siege of Rouen he was born an Englishman, but by the time he started buying property he was French. Although originally from Norman stock, my ancestors must have been confused over the years as to what nationality they actually were. The city had changed hands so frequently, being at first Norman, then English, then French, then English, and finally French.

Jehan was also a burgess and became a wealthy man, as is demonstrated by his proclivity for buying and selling property. He started accumulating buildings and land in 1461 when he invested in a house in Lacroix-Saint-Ouen complete with outbuildings, a well, and gardens from Jehan Bernard. Not content with this, seven years later he procured a hostel recognised by the sign of The Stone from Guillaume Le Carpentier and Geoffroy Marc – most buildings had a sign hanging at the entrance which had some significance to the owner, as many people did not know how to read. The property had outbuildings, a cellar, a courtyard and stables, and was situated in rue aux Pelletiers in Lacroix-Saint-Ouen. Jehan sold this, presumably for a profit, eleven years later to Raoul La Pelle.

Another addition was an orchard and garden in Saint-Éloi, which he bought in 1476 and sold two years later. In the same year Jehan invested in a residence, 'where hangs the sign of a Crowned Crow', situated in the parish of Saint-Vincent. He also purchased a basement of another house to the rear of the Crowned Crow, which was separated by an alley, together with a small stable and garden, 'where hangs the sign of a Cygnet'. Jehan's final acquisitions were in 1503 when he invested in five *verges* – roughly 1.25 acres – of enclosed ground in Saint-Étienne, and a dwelling and plot in Caumont, adjacent to the chapel in the hamlet of La Bouille. He bought the latter from a ranger Guillaume Vieil, who lived in the Forest of La Londe. This holding remained in the family until his grandsons Pierre and Denys sold it twenty years later.

At some stage Jehan moved from Saint-Éloi to nearby Saint-Vincent, where the family remained until he died. Despite his quest to obtain property, Jehan found the time to marry twice. The name of his first wife is unknown. In 1467 he married Pierette, widow of Thibault Amyot, but his first wife was the mother of his daughter, Jehanne, and sons Jehan and Denys II.

In the fifteenth century people were enthralled with macabre events. The Le Plastriers kept some records regarding accidental killings, which contain some rather gory but fascinating glimpses into the life of ordinary people. For instance, a local inhabitant Guillaume Morin was stuffing himself with food in preparation for the Lent fast. When he had finished eating his meat, he threw the bone out of the window. Unfortunately, his young daughter was staggering back from the tavern with more wine for the family at the time, and the bone fell on her head and killed her.

Another account is that of a favourite game played at Christmas, in which lumps of wood were thrown at a goose tied by its leg to a tall pole; the idea being that whoever killed the goose could keep it for their Christmas dinner. When it was the turn of Jacques Basqueler, he missed his shot and hit his friend Lavalloys on the temple, killing him instead of the goose. A few years later, a stay-maker – corset maker – was unable to help her customer Marie Mansel with the fit of her stays. Exasperated, Marie clouted the poor stay-maker so hard that she died within a few days.

In the same year, a butcher complained that his hair had been cut too short in a barber's shop in Lacroix-Saint-Ouen. He was so vexed that when he met the barber the next day, he 'smote him one, and ran.' However, the barber Nicolas Courtil ran faster, caught the butcher, and killed him with the instrument of his trade, his scissors. Another story is that of Louis de Houdetot, a priest, who had been so successful in seducing Madame Tilleran that her husband sent her out of town to her father's house. This did not deter the priest, who continued the good work. When the outraged husband became aware of this, he sallied forth armed with a crossbow. On finding the priest hiding in a side street in Rouen, he shot him.

In the interim, exciting events were happening in the world, such as the discovery of America by Christopher Columbus in 1492, and in 1498 Vasco da Gama discovered the route round the Cape of Good Hope to India and the Spice Islands. France was also experiencing its fair share of upheaval and change, and Jehan and his family lived through the turbulent times of dual monarchy, the appearance of Joan of Arc, and the continuing war with England.

Henry VI's regents, his uncles the dukes of Bedford and Gloucester, were determined to have the infant crowned king of France as soon as possible. Meanwhile, the rightful king, the dauphin, Charles, having been disinherited by his mad father in favour of Henry V and his heirs, was in a desperate position. As the English and their allies, the

Burgundians, had captured most of northern France leaving Charles with very few territories, he was forced to move his court to Bourges, south of the Loire River, which was one of the few remaining areas left for him to rule. He was now known as 'the king of Bourges' by the English and the Burgundians.

Charles was married to Marie d'Anjou, but, despite their fourteen children, his affections were given to his favourite mistress Agnès Sorel, known as *Dame de beauté*, with whom he fathered three daughters. Marie's mother was the formidable Yolande d'Aragon. She was instrumental in introducing her son-in-law to Joan of Arc, thereby ensuring Charles's eventual ascendance to the throne, and ultimately helping to end the Hundred Years' War.

The country's political and military position was dramatically enhanced when seventeen-year-old Jehanne d'Arc, better known as Joan of Arc, 'the Maid', became the spiritual leader of France. She was a simple peasant girl born in Domrémy on the border of Champagne and Lorraine, and was the daughter of a farmer Jacques d'Arc and his wife, Isabelle Romée. With her strong faith, and apparent gift of a divine mission, she assisted her country in winning some important battles against the English. People were fascinated by mystics, particularly if they purported to hear predictions from God through the medium of angels.

At the time several prophecies were circulating, one of which declared that France had been ruined by a woman, possibly a reference to Charles's mother, the avaricious Isabeau, but would be restored by a virgin from Lorraine. Joan was certain that this referred to her, as she had started 'hearing voices' when she was a young girl. The first voice she heard was that of St Michael the Archangel, who in the heavenly hierarchy of saints was the leader and protector against evil. She later heard those of St Margaret and St Catherine. They all insisted that Charles would one day become king and that she must lead him to his coronation.

During her trial, when recounting St Michael's messages, she told the court, 'The voice told me that I should make my way to Robert de Baudricourt in the fortress of Vaucouleurs, the Captain of that place, that he would give me people to go with me.'[2] He was in charge of an Armagnac garrison stationed there and received his military instructions from Yolande's son René d'Anjou. He was, therefore, Joan's best means of eventually reaching the dauphin, as she always referred to Charles. Determined to obey the voices, she persuaded her relative Durand Laxart and his wife to take her to the nearby town, which was loyal to the dauphin. While staying there she managed to meet Baudricourt and explain the voices to him.

Faced with the young peasant girl, dressed in a rough red serge surcoat and cap, talking about voices from angels, was too much for the hardened soldier who treated her with contempt and disbelief. This conversation was heard by many of the townspeople, who believed Joan and were convinced that she was divinely blessed. A bystander reported, 'Joan the Maid came to Vaucouleurs at the time of the Ascension of Our Lord, as I recall it, and there I saw her speak with Robert de Baudricourt, who was then the Captain of the town. She told him that she was come to him, Robert, sent by her Lord to bring word to the Dauphin…'[3]

Having failed to convince him on their first meeting, she returned to the town six months later, again with the help of Durand Laxart, but was still unable to get noticed. Determined to win Baudricourt over, she decided to remain and found lodgings with a couple named Henri and Catherine Le Royer. Joan had always been interested in observing soldiers prepare for battle, and during her stay she took every opportunity to familiarise herself with army practice. The townsfolk were in awe of her, and she eventually became widely respected and revered as a genuine soothsayer and holy woman.

The vitally important, beautiful walled city of Orléans was under siege by the English at the time. If it fell into their hands it would be disastrous. Something had to be done, and fast. Charles was ineffectual and weak, so it fell to his indomitable mother-in-law Yolande to raise an army. Her aspirations were to see her son-in-law crowned king, to ensure that her lands were secure, and that the duchies of Bar and Lorraine should pass into the hands of her younger son René. However, the dauphin refused to declare war to save Orléans, maintaining that he was waiting for a sign from God. Word had reached Yolande of Joan's persistent claims, and this is when everything started to fall into place for her, for the dauphin, and unknowingly for Joan, who became an innocent pawn in a dangerous political scheme. Charles's biographer M. G. A. Vale wrote, 'To introduce a prophetess to the impressionable Charles could have been a stroke of something approaching political genius. Who could have considered such a step both necessary and desirable?'[4]

Yolande was convinced that Joan was, as she claimed, the Maid of the divinations. She had captivated the ailing Duc de Lorraine, René's father-in-law, and endured being questioned by a priest to ensure that the voices she heard were good and not bad voices – a procedure known as 'the discernment of spirits.' Probably on instructions from Yolande, Baudricourt finally began to believe, or was ordered to believe, that Joan really did hear voices from God, as he seemingly had a sudden change of heart. He unexpectedly called at the Le Royers' home to inform her that he was prepared to provide men to guide her safely through the dangerous countryside to Chinon, where Charles and the court were residing. Joan recalled, 'Robert twice refused and repulsed me, and the third time he received me and gave me men. The voice told me that it would happen so.'[5]

The proud townsfolk gathered to help the Maid prepare for the perilous journey, and the long-awaited meeting with the dauphin. They even bought her a horse. Her simple clothes were discarded, her hair cropped and, at Joan's request, she was dressed in dark-coloured men's attire consisting of tunic, doublet, hose, breeches, and a black woollen cap. It is understandable that she preferred to dress as a man as it was imperative that she remained a virgin. The voices had promised that a Maid – a virgin – would save the kingdom. She was in serious danger of being raped, regardless of the promised safe conduct and her holy persona, as she would be living and sleeping among illiterate and crude men-at-arms during her journey.

Joan left for Chinon on 12 February 1429. She later affirmed, 'Robert de Baudricourt caused those who escorted me to swear that they would lead me truly and surely.'[6] True to their word, after a hazardous journey travelling through forests and dangerous enemy territory, they arrived safely at Chinon eleven days later where Joan found lodgings in a *hostellerie* in rue Saint-Maurice. It is widely recognised that Yolande and her allies were now protecting and funding the Maid. Despite opposition from many courtiers, the Compte de Vendôme eventually led her to the castle for an audience with Charles.

The unworldly young girl must have been totally overawed on entering the fabulous Great Hall, where hundreds of pages holding flaming torches stood in front of magnificent tapestries. Courtiers floated around gracefully in splendid furs and silks. Ladies wore the grand costumes of the day with tall headdresses from which hung long, trailing festoons of cloth of gold emblazoned with jewels, their robes richly embroidered with their family coat of arms. Charles, hoping for some divine hint, was deliberately disguised as one of the many courtiers. Joan, who could not have known what he looked like, walked serenely into the hall where they were assembled, and without any hesitation fell on her knees before him.

Raoul de Gaucourt, a royal councillor, recounted, 'I was myself present at the castle and the city of Chinon when the Maid arrived, and I saw her when she presented herself to his Royal Majesty. She showed great humility and simplicity of manner, this poor little shepherdess... '[7] It is not known how she managed to win the trust of the dauphin and persuade him of her divine gift, but it is thought that among other signs she gave him confirmation that he was the legitimate heir to his father's throne – it had long been rumoured that he may have been the bastard son of his uncle and mother's lover, the murdered Louis d'Orléans.

After their meeting Charles seemed more confident and eager to fight the English, which delighted Yolande and her allies, but not some of the dauphin's intimate advisors such as the shrewd Georges de La

Trémoille. They were pro-Burgundian and could see their power and riches endangered if Joan was successful. Although Charles believed in her he also listened to advice from his priests and councillors, who all had conflicting views. Many were sceptical and undecided whether the Maid was sent from heaven or hell. The atmosphere was charged with suspicion, as politically many obstacles had to be overcome before any decisions could be made. La Trémoille and his allies did not trust her but Yolande and her adherents, who had so much to lose if the English captured Orléans, were determined to risk letting her lead her men into battle.

Joan remained impatiently in Chinon, living in the Great Keep of the tower of the castle with a guard and maidservants for company. She spent her time in prayer and practised riding and wielding her lance, while one faction argued with the other, and Charles was as usual indecisive and ineffective. It was eventually decided to send her to Poitiers – the administrative centre of Bourges – for more cross-examining. She was interrogated by clerics for three weeks before they announced her to be genuinely holy, pure, and a virgin. At last, she was free to carry out her calling and relieve the occupation of Orléans.

Riding a white war horse, and proudly holding her colourful banner high above her, Joan set off from Blois with her men-at-arms for her first battle. She was accompanied by her many loyal disciples including her almoner, heralds, and priests. Her once sceptical, tough and seasoned troops were now completely under her spell and willingly stopped to pray with her between battles. She carried a sword with five crosses scratched upon it that she had found, rusty and neglected, behind the altar in the Church of Sainte-Catherine, while passing through the small town of Sainte-Catherine-de-Fierbois. She treated this sword as her sacred weapon.

Although Joan never actually fought in a battle, or killed anyone, she was responsible for outlining military strategies and directing her troops. She and her army miraculously delivered Orléans from the English in just nine days and continued to capture other important towns and cities. This paved the way for Charles VII to be crowned in July 1429 at Rheims Cathedral. The Maid, dressed in shining armour and holding her banner, stood proudly by his side. The coronation and Joan's success at Orléans boosted the morale of the French, as hostilities and battles continued. Charles was known as *le Victorieux*, and Joan and her family were rewarded with status and gifts. Civil war still raged between the Armagnacs who supported Charles, and the Burgundians who supported Henry VI. Unfortunately, Joan's power diminished when she failed to take Paris and other major towns, and the king and his subjects began to lose faith in her. She was now accused by many of hearing the devil's voices rather than those from God through angels.

While the king enjoyed his new-found success, the dukes of Bedford and Gloucester together with Cardinal Henry Beaufort were desperate to see young Henry crowned king of France as soon as possible. They were most perturbed when Joan was discovered, and the French won so many key battles. Determined to destroy her, they enlisted the help of their allies the Burgundians who were only too happy to oblige. On 24 May 1430, Joan was captured in Compiègne and sold to the English for ten thousand *livres**. They made use of this precious gift for their own ends by accusing her of heresy and dressing as a man. She was taken in chains to the Château de Rouen, where she was imprisoned in an iron cage before being charged and tried. She did not stand a chance of proving herself innocent. The proceedings were established from the start, and her judges paid handsomely to find her guilty.

They were mainly pro-English doctors and prelates, but the prime instigators were Cardinal Beaufort and Pierre Cauchon, bishop of Beauvais. The latter hoped to become Archbishop of Rouen by winning this case. He carefully chose the jury and other officials, who he knew would ensure that he got the verdict he wanted, but he never reached his goal for he died of apoplexy shortly after Joan's death. The Maid's only crime was that she never wavered in her belief that she

---

*   *Livre* - a unit equal to one pound of silver

heard voices from God telling her that her beloved homeland must be liberated from English domination, and that the dauphin should be crowned king. Her accusers kept her imprisoned, but they were unable to break her will.

By resorting to torture, a last attempt was made to coerce Joan into admitting that the voices had misled her and that her mission was untrue. Defeated, she signed a confession denying that she had ever received divine guidance. Several days later she regained her conviction, repudiated her previous confession, and reverted to donning men's clothing. She explained that she did this to prevent the soldiers from raping her while she was imprisoned. This was a very real fear as they were on the whole lawless men who despised and tortured her and, arguably, did indeed attempt to rape her. The judges now abandoned any semblance of justice, and Cauchon delivered the verdict. Joan was guilty of heresy. She was to be burned alive by purifying fire. When Beaufort refused to lodge her appeal for clemency with the pope, and she heard that she was to be burned at the stake the following day, she cried out in horror:

> *Alas! Do they treat me thus horribly and cruelly, so that my body, clean and whole, which was never corrupted, must be this day consumed and reduced to ashes… Alas! Had I been in the ecclesiastical prison to which I submitted myself and been guarded by men of the Church and not by my enemies and adversaries, it had not so wretchedly happened to me as now it has! Ah! I appeal before God, the Great Judge, from the great wrongs and grievances being done to me.*[8]

As she entered the dungeon after her conviction, she called out accusingly to Cauchon, 'Bishop, I die by you!'[9] Despite everything that she had done for the king and the people of France, extraordinarily, no attempt was made to save her. On 30 May 1431, eight hundred soldiers, laughing, and carrying blades and axes, led the terrified and bitterly weeping young woman to the Place du Marché – the marketplace – where she was tied to an extremely tall pillar so that all of Rouen could witness her fate. Crowds gathered several feet deep, while others hung out of windows, many jeering and shouting, 'Whore!' and 'Heretic!' Others knelt, holding lighted candles, weeping and praying.

The Maid, who had so bravely led her soldiers into battle and endured *arquebus** fire and cannonballs, succumbed to the terror that lay before her and broke down, sobbing uncontrollably. After being kept waiting for six hours as ecclesiastics preached sermons on the evils of heresy, it took almost forty minutes for her to die, as she repeatedly implored the saints of paradise to help her. One of the soldiers took pity on her and held a hastily and crudely made wooden crucifix before her, while the crowd wept with her as she slowly burned to death. Many of the jury later admitted that they had voted in fear of their lives, as few dared to oppose the influential Cauchon.

Jehan and his family almost certainly witnessed the trial and tragic death of Joan, as burnings and executions were a form of entertainment and everyone turned out to watch the spectacle. I am sure that my ancestors would have been among those who were kneeling, praying, and holding candles in sorrow and respect.

The English were wrong in thinking they could break the morale of the French by capturing Joan and burning her for heresy. She became a patriotic heroine and was ultimately beatified in 1909 and canonised a saint in 1920 at St Peter's Basilica. Every year on 30 May a feast day is celebrated in memory of the Maid with a symbolic burning in a huge urn in what is now called the Place du Vieux Marché – the Old Market Place.

In December, shortly after Joan's death, ten-year-old King Henry VI dressed in scarlet and ermine robes and accompanied by his uncles the dukes of Bedford and Gloucester, and a retinue of aristocratic courtiers, was crowned king of France at Notre-Dame in Paris. There were now two kings ruling one country. Unlike his father, he was a vacuous and feeble king who was disinclined to warfare, and the English lost most of the battles undertaken during his sovereignty. He

---

* *Arquebus* – an early muzzle-loaded musket.

was not popular in either country, as he was forced to continue raising taxes in order to pay for futile conflicts. Dual monarchy eventually ended following the final French victory at the Battle of Castillon in 1453, thus bringing an end to the Hundred Years' War and the English were banished from all areas of France except Calais.

Charles VII reigned successfully for thirty years. Latterly his reign was impaired by his tempestuous relationship with his son Louis XI, who ascended the throne in 1461. Louis was nicknamed *le Ruse* – the Cunning – due to his many plots, intrigues, and frenetic diplomatic activity. He was married to Margaret of Scotland when thirteen and she only eleven, in an arranged marriage which was not successful. Margaret died childless. Louis's second wife, and the mother of the future king Charles VIII, was Charlotte de Savoie. The death of Louis's enemy Charles the Bold at the Battle of Nancy in 1477 boosted his popularity as it finally ended the powerful dynasty of the dukes of Burgundy, enabling Louis to seize numerous Burgundian territories, thereby strengthening the economy and his sovereignty.

CHAPTER FOUR

Onset Of The Persecution Of The Huguenots

Personal and family piety was still sustained and strengthened by prayers.[1]

H. M. Baird

Jean Calvin was born in 1509 in Noyon, Picardy. He was the son of a lawyer who was also secretary to the Bishop of Noyon. It was through the influence of his father that Calvin was appointed a cathedral chaplain at the age of twelve. Subsequently, he trained as a humanist lawyer and was introduced to the 'New Religion' by his cousin Pierre Robert Olivétan.* This made such an impression on him that he broke away from the Catholic Church.

After the death of his father, Calvin followed his dream and studied theology, eventually becoming an influential theologian and pastor of

---

* Pierre Robert Olivétan [c. 1506–1538] was one of the first to translate the Bible into French starting from the Hebrew and Greek texts. He was a Waldensian by faith – a pre-Protestant movement founded by Peter Waldo c. 1173.

the Protestant Church. He rejected the idea of Mass being held in Latin, preferring the service to be conducted in the vernacular. He also disliked the pomp and ceremony of the Catholic Church and was suspicious of the pope and some of the priests, who he believed were corrupt. Calvin preached the doctrine of predestination, which later helped the Huguenots to stand firm in the face of torture and death. However, it seems strange that having successfully converted so many Catholics, on seeing how dangerous it was to be a 'heretic' in France he fled to Basel in Switzerland, leaving his flock to cope with the dangers.

He laid down the laws governing the constitution of the Protestant Church, which still exist. Ministers and elders later formed the consistory, supervising the lives of the congregation in the individual churches and disciplining their shortcomings. This led to reformed morals and a purposeful way of life. 'It is said that all the Huguenot men in Rouen produced far fewer bastards than one king of France.'[2]

Denys, son of Jehan, the entrepreneur, was born in 1465. He lived with his wife, Agnes Goudart, and their four children including my ancestor Denys III in the parish of Saint-Vincent on the outskirts of the city. He was *Sergent du Roy la vicomte de l'eau de Rouen*, which meant that he dealt with all the legal and taxation complications relevant to the vast maritime trade that took place there. It was an important and prestigious position appointed by the Duke of Normandy or the king.

Denys III was the first Le Plastrier to follow the teachings of Calvin and desert the Catholic faith. An educated, deep-thinking and intelligent merchant, he was dismayed by some of the unscrupulous practices that were occurring in the Catholic Church, and despised the cult of relics. The Calvinist philosophy of frugality, humility, integrity, and diligence appealed to his puritanical and intellectual nature. He also felt more comfortable making his peace with God, rather than being given absolution by a duplicitous priest. It cannot have been an easy commitment for him to make, or for his wife, Ester Fessart, and three sons Jehan, Denys, and Symon who were all devout Catholics, but they were duty-bound to follow his decision. The family became early devotees and remained resolute Protestants for the rest of their lives.

It was the custom for people practising different professions to live in designated streets such as rue des Tapissiers – the Tapestry Makers' Street, or rue aux Pelletiers – the Furriers' Street. Later, a royal decree specified that all Rouen goldsmiths must live in the prestigious rue du Gros Horloge near Notre-Dame, then called rue Courvoiserie.

Denys owned a successful business involving trading. It was extremely difficult for Huguenots to operate any sort of enterprise during these perilous times, and not surprisingly, the business eventually suffered. His eldest son Jehan, who became a goldsmith in 1560 and moved into a grand house in rue du Gros Horloge, as stipulated, desperately tried to keep the company afloat by borrowing money from other merchants. He was unfortunately killed during the uprisings, and before he was able to complete the payments. His younger brothers Symon and Denys were unable to continue paying the interest at that stage, and the business was foreclosed and sold to Claude de Presbestre, a rich merchant of Paris.

Their father never recovered financially from this loss and died leaving a deficit in his personal estate of 560 *livres*. This was eventually paid by Robert Rouelle, husband of Denys's widow Ester, and reflects the deep loyalty Huguenots felt for each other and their families. My ancestor Symon ultimately became a wealthy, influential master goldsmith and merchant, but too late to help his father. Colonel H. A. Du Pont says of the Le Plastriers in his book, *The Early Generations of the Du Pont and Allied Families*, 'Some of them were accounted very rich as measured by the standards of those days.'[3] Although the Le Plastriers were prominent and devout Protestants, unlike some they were never militant. All they wanted was to practise their new religion in peace, but they were regarded with suspicion and distrust. Like so many others, they were thrown unawares into the turmoil and slaughter that occurred under the rule of François I and his successors. All were responsible for the persecution of Huguenots.

François was the son of Charles, Compte d'Angoulême, and Louise de Savoie. He and his sister, Marguerite, spent their childhood at Château d'Amboise, and François maintained his residence there in the early days of his sovereignty. Marguerite lived nearby as the siblings were very close. Her second husband was Henri, king of the principality of Navarre, a small vassal state in the foothills of the Pyrenees near the Spanish border. They had one surviving child, a daughter, Jeanne d'Albret, who eventually became an inspired leading Huguenot. Marguerite was a talented poet and playwriter, and a popular and influential philanthropist. She spent her life mediating between the Catholics and the Protestants and saving many of the latter from being burned at the stake. When Protestantism was in its infancy, she gave Huguenots sanctuary in the principality of Navarre.

François was married to Claude, Duchess of Brittany, the mild and devout mother of his seven children. He succeeded his cousin and father-in-law Louis XII, who died in 1515 without having produced an heir. At the time of his death Louis was married to his third wife, the beautiful princess, Mary Tudor, sister of Henry VIII. Anne Boleyn and her sister, also called Mary, accompanied the princess when she arrived in France the year before to marry the much older king. The marriage was negotiated by Cardinal Wolsey in 1514 as part of the Anglo-French Peace Treaty, and lasted less than three months.

After the death of her husband, Mary returned to England and married Charles Brandon, Duke of Suffolk, and Anne was invited to remain as one of Queen Claude's attendants. Although far from beautiful, she was popular with the queen and courtiers for her vivacious personality, grace, and sense of style. She also developed a close friendship with the king's sister, and under her influence began to embrace the teachings of Calvin. While living at the opulent, decadent French court Anne also learned her chic, sophisticated, and beguiling ways which later led to her capturing the heart of Henry VIII, and ultimately causing him to break with Rome and declare himself head of the Church of England.

François was a large man, over six feet tall, and possessed a commanding, imposing, and charismatic personality. He loved fine clothes and presented a resplendent figure in his black and gold satin doublet, encrusted with pearls and lined with ermine. Each finger sparkled with further precious jewels. He was known as *François du Grand Nez* because he had an extremely long nose, and *le Père et Restaurateur des Lettres* for his role in standardising the French language.

Queen Claude died in 1524 and he later married Eleanor of Castile, who remained childless. The pleasure-loving king was passionate about hunting, falconry, wrestling, jousts, swordplay, and risqué masked balls. He surrounded himself with beautiful women of all classes, known as *La Petite Bande*. These beguiling young ladies were expected to amuse, soothe, entertain, and sleep with him when required. He set the tone for one of the most debauched courts of the period.

In the Renaissance the whiter the skin, the lighter the hair, the more beautiful a lady was considered. Natural blondes were the epitome of beauty and highly sought after. This tempted many women with darker hair to use dyes, made from different coloured flowers, crushed and mixed into a powder with a glue-like substance. Others opted to hide their locks under fashionable pearl-rimmed hoods, or elaborate gem-encrusted bands displaying majesty and prosperity. A pomander usually made of gold or silver and divided into partitions, each containing a different perfume such as ambergris and musk, was used to protect themselves from infection and unpleasant smells. The spherical cases concealing them were hung from a neck-chain, belt, or attached to the girdle.

White lead-based powder, sometimes laced with mercury, was applied to smooth and beautify their faces. The ingredients were of course extremely toxic if not used sparingly. High foreheads and pale eyebrows were also desirable, and hair was frequently cut or tweezed before being pumiced to achieve the desired, smooth effect. Ladies of wealth and high social rank typically chose expensive materials such as brocades, silks, and heavy velvet, abundantly trimmed with jewels. Long skirts were wide and supported with hoops. Low necklines, adorned with ruffles and fine lace from Brussels, accentuated the curve of a lady's chest. Undergarments, such as kirtles, chemises, and pantaloons, sometimes consisting of up to four layers, were equally fine and exquisitely embroidered.

As well as beautiful women and hunting, François was an avid reader, writer, and poet. He was also a patron of the arts and enjoyed the company of talented artists, especially the charismatic Leonardo da Vinci who introduced him to the Renaissance. The king was so taken with Leonardo that he gave him Manoir du Cloux, now named Château du Clos Lucé, which was connected to Château d'Amboise by an underground passage. He also bought the *Mona Lisa – La Gioconda* – from him. This wonderful painting remained with the royal family for many years, moving from one château to another. It now hangs in its rightful place, the Louvre. François employed Italian artists to renovate his many châteaux, including the enormous and opulent Château de Blois and the Château de Saint-Germain-en-Laye, about ten miles northwest of Paris. He also transformed the Louvre from a medieval fortress into a splendid palace to use as his main Paris residence. Leonardo remained close to the king until his death at the age of sixty-seven in 1519, while at Manoir du Cloux. It is said that the king was so devoted to him that he held his head as he was dying.

François's reign saw the beginning of the French exploration of the New World and the expansion of the first French Colonial Empire. It also saw the swift spread of Protestantism, and consequently terrible acts of violence towards the Huguenots.

Although more interested in the arts and beautiful women than fighting wars, the king still found time to persist with the Great Italian Wars, started by his predecessors. The Holy Roman Emperor, Charles V, a vassal of the Vatican, whose extensive realm included Austria, Spain, the Netherlands, and large sections of Italy, was a lifelong enemy. In February 1525 François led his army into battle against Charles, but was defeated in Pavia, captured by the Spanish troops, and imprisoned by the emperor.

Humiliated, and to extricate himself from the hardship of being confined in the dungeons of a grim castle, he agreed to sign the Treaty of Madrid the following year renouncing claims to Burgundy, Italy, and Flanders, but he had no intention of complying. Charles V suspected this, and to ensure that the king would not renege insisted that his two eldest sons, the eight-year-old dauphin François and his six-year-old brother Henri d'Orléans – later Henri II – be substituted as hostages.

As expected, the king did break his word and the two boys spent four miserable years incarcerated in the dark, damp cells of a castle in Spain, never knowing what the future held for them, or when, and if, they would be released. After much mediating, and huge ransoms had been paid, both boys were finally freed. Marguerite played a large part in negotiating the release of her brother, and eventually that of his sons.

In 1533 Henri married the plain, bulgy-eyed Catherine de'Medici from the wealthy but socially inferior ruling family of Florence, when both were only fourteen. She married under the Gallicised version of her name, de Médicis. Her parents were Lorenzo de'Medici, Duke of Urbino, and Madeleine de La Tour d'Auvergne, a cousin of François. The young couple died within six days of each other when Catherine was only three weeks old. It was said that both died of syphilis, Madeleine having caught it from her husband, but it is more likely that she died from puerperal fever due to childbirth.

A new mother was always at risk from this pernicious fever, which could strike at any time during the postpartum period. Their daughter became the responsibility of her extended family and led a sad and lonely childhood. It was spent between the sumptuous splendour of Florentine palaces and various grim convents, depending on the rise and fall of the House of Medici. Her uncle Pope Clement VII eventually arranged for her marriage to Henri, proudly calling it 'the greatest match in the world.'[4]

Catherine brought a substantial dowry to the kingdom, including priceless jewellery to add to the crown jewel collection; the most famous being some huge, natural pear-shaped pearls which were said to be 'worth a kingdom.'[5] The marriage was a useful alliance with Rome and François's long-standing nemesis the Holy Roman Emperor. The wedding was held at the Église Saint-Ferréol les Augustines in Marseille with festivities and feasts lasting thirty-four days.

As Henri was next in line to the throne after his brother, it was of constitutional importance that he was capable of producing an heir. Thus, at midnight Catherine and Henri retired to their huge, canopied, nuptial bed in their luxurious chamber, romantically lit by tall beeswax candles. After Clement had blessed the bed, the king, queen, and others of the inner sanctum remained in the young couple's bedchamber until they were quite sure that the marriage had been suitably consummated. The pope could not hide his elation and 'late that night, and early the next morning, he entered the bridal chamber, trembling with secular anxiety, to see with his own eyes the daughter of the Medici covered by the son of the Valois.'[6] There was little privacy for royalty, especially monarchs, who were expected to perform the most intimate acts in the presence of personal servants and courtiers. They were never alone for a moment.

A pragmatist, and under the influence of his beloved sister, François was initially relatively tolerant of Protestants. His policy was that it was acceptable for them to practise their beliefs in private but if the heretics dared to cross the invisible line, it was treason. The peasants, particularly in Paris, thought differently. They loathed the misunderstood Huguenots and tormented them at every opportunity – the cruelty of the Paris mob was legendary. Ercole Strozzi, an Italian banker, says of them, 'These people are so exasperated against those of the New Religion that, if they find one of them anywhere, they slay him without more ado, and drag him through the place as though he was a dog.'[7]

Despite his putative liberality, François turned a blind eye to the shocking victimisation that was carried out on innocent converts. Consequently, on 17 and 18 October 1534 in despair at their barbaric treatment some of the most influential Huguenots, allegedly led by a pastor named Antoine de Marcourt, distributed anti-Catholic pamphlets in the major cities of Rouen, Blois, Tours, and Orléans.

The king was enraged and surprised when, during the night a pamphlet was placed in his handkerchief box on his bedchamber door at Château d'Amboise. He felt personally threatened by this insult, especially as in his opinion he had always been reasonably lenient. He considered this a crime of *lèse-majesté* and showed his displeasure by taking an active part with the Sorbonne* to identify the guilty heretics. All were condemned to death. He personally attended the public executions of the culprits, who were burned alive in front of Notre-Dame in Paris. This incident became known as the *Affaire des Placards.*

The king's attitude had now changed from toleration to issuing the Edict of Fontainebleau in 1540, which stated that Protestantism was heresy and therefore treason punishable by torture, loss of property and goods, public humiliation, and death by burning. Nobles were given the honour of being decapitated by sword, their heads later paraded around cities and towns on pikes, eyes staring accusingly out of their sockets. It is not known if any Le Plastriers suffered, but there is no doubt that it must have been a terrifying time for them. It was particularly dangerous for those living in Paris or Rouen.

The edict resulted in hundreds of Huguenots, and suspected sympathisers, being horribly murdered or left homeless. Several prominent Protestant leaders, including John Calvin, fled in fear of their lives. Later, Calvin moved to Geneva from where, with the help of trusted agents, he began sending preachers to France to spread the new doctrine and sell Protestant literature and bibles printed in Geneva. They took enormous risks, as if discovered the penalty was death.

Huguenots were on the whole peaceful people, who referred to themselves as belonging to *l'Église Réformée* – the Reformed Church, and followers of the true gospel. They dressed in sombre shades of black and grey and lived modest, hard-working lives. If caught discussing their faith, chanting psalms, or reading bibles in French instead of Latin, they were tortured and burned alive. It was considered heresy. Thus, they congregated secretly in obscure places

---

* In the sixteenth century the Sorbonne, the University of Paris, largely devoted its attentions to destroying Huguenots.

such as caves and cowsheds to pray, hold meetings, and discuss the scriptures.

The dauphin died in 1536 aged eighteen; probably from tuberculosis caused by the years spent in the damp dungeons of the castle in Spain, and his younger brother Henri became heir apparent. It was rumoured that the dauphin may have been poisoned by one of Catherine's Italian servants, so that Henri would succeed their father rather than his elder brother. A death amongst royalty or the nobility was automatically assumed to be by poisoning. Murder at court was a common occurrence which usually went unpunished.

Although Catherine's father hailed from the so-called common merchant class, she was at first regarded with interest by the snobbish, class-conscious courtiers for her intelligence and the wealth she brought to their kingdom. This changed on the death of Clement, as Pope Paul III repudiated the papal alliance with France and most of the agreed dowry never materialised. François bemoaned, '*J'ai reçu la fille toute nue.*'[8] – put simply, the girl has come to my court stark naked. Catherine hero-worshipped her father-in-law, who towards the end of his life had learnt to respect and admire her for her courage and love of hunting. She also became very friendly with the daughter of Marguerite, Jeanne d'Albret, whose second husband was Antoine de Bourbon. Both became Huguenots.

Regardless of her heavy features and protruding eyes, Catherine was accepted into the king's exclusive *La Petite Bande.* Membership was strictly vetted by François's 'declared mistress' Anne d'Heilly, Duchesse d'Étampes. Admittance normally required beauty of face and body, good repartee, and an enjoyment of rowdy, licentious banquets and vulgar gossip, but most importantly skilled horsemanship. Catherine certainly possessed the latter requirement if not the others.

Riding was her passion, and she later lavished a fortune on her stables and horses. Pierre de Bourdeïlle, Seigneur de Brantôme, soldier and court chronicler – commonly referred to as Brantôme – wrote of her, 'She was very good on horseback, and bold, sitting with ease, and being the first to put her leg around a pommel, which was far more graceful and becoming than sitting with the feet upon a plank.' He also noted that 'if the king played at *pall-mall* [rather like croquet] she watched him play and played herself. She was very fond of shooting with a crossbow à *jalet* [ball of stone] and she shot right well; so that always when she went to ride her crossbow was taken with her, and if she saw any game, she shot it.'[9]

Catherine's initial inability to have a child, and lack of the promised dowry, did not sit well with some of the courtiers who treated her with disdain and endless humiliation. The influential and ambitious Huguenot-hating Guise family made no secret of their dislike of her and fought to depose her when she was having difficulty conceiving. The Guises were a junior branch of the House of Lorraine, an independent imperial duchy. They ridiculed her foreign accent and Anna d'Este, the arrogant wife of François, Duc de Guise, wrote that the Medici were 'tradesmen who are not fit to call themselves our servants.'[10] Who would have thought then that Catherine would be remembered as one of the most powerful women in Europe, whose determination and tenacity dominated the fortunes of France for more than a quarter of a century. Huguenot descendants think of her rather differently.

Soon after his marriage, Henri fell for the charms of thirty-five-year-old Diane de Poitiers, Duchesse de Valentinois, and remained devoted to her throughout his reign. Henri had known Diane, an alluring, elegant, aloof aristocratic widow, since he was a child as his father had also admired her. He sported her favourite black-and-white colours at jousts and wore priceless, sparkling jewels encrusted in the helmet of his elaborate armour. At the end of a successful contest, he pulled them off and flung them at his mistress to show his adoration. He kept her constantly at his side, intermittently fondling her breasts, or strumming his cither, while discussing important matters of state with foreign dignitaries.

During this period Catherine was engrossed in attempting to produce a child. She did not take any interest in the politics and scheming that occurred at court, unlike Henri's much older mistress. Emboldened by her influence and knowing that the king disliked sleeping with his wife, Diane insisted that he continue to do so in order to produce an heir and spares. Regardless of the age difference, Diane and Henri remained close and shared a bed until he died. It is said that she would start making love to him, but at the optimal moment send him to his wife where he did his duty before returning to her. According to Brantôme, Catherine, whose bedchamber was directly above her adversary in one of their many châteaux, had a secret panel cut into the floor so that she could spy on their lovemaking. Diane was not only Henri's mistress, but the power behind the throne. It was widely accepted that she took precedence over his wife in many cases. She was also an ally of the Guises, and responsible for many of the atrocities suffered by the Huguenots.

Despite placing poultices of cow dung and ground stags' antlers on her 'source of life', drinking mules' urine, and wearing a locket stuffed with a cremated frog, it was ten years before Catherine produced her first child. There had been talk of divorce due to her apparent inability to conceive, and in desperation a physician was summoned to examine the couple. He found that both their reproductive organs revealed small physical abnormalities and suggested a method to overcome them.

This was successful as her first child and heir, François, was born in January 1544 at Fontainebleau. She went on to have ten children; seven of whom survived, with three of them becoming future kings: François II, Charles d'Orléans, later Charles IX, and Henri d'Anjou, later Henri III. Her other surviving children were Elisabeth de Valois, later queen of Spain; Claude de Valois, François d'Alençon,[*] and Marguerite de Valois, who became queen of Navarre, and ultimately queen of France. Almost all grew up to be corrupt, cruel, and scheming. Diane deliberately befriended Catherine, and later spent many hours with her and her children in their private chambers.

---

[*]   François d'Alençon's birth name was Hercule François, but he changed it to François. Much later he became Duc d'Anjou. .

Much earlier, when his wife was struggling to conceive, Henri proved his manhood by fathering a daughter by a beautiful Piedmontese girl, Filippa Duci. He later legitimised her and gave her the name Diane de France – behind her back she was known as *Madame Bâtarde*. She was named after Diane de Poitiers who became responsible for the upbringing of her namesake, while the child's mother spent the remainder of her years incarcerated in a convent.

François died, after a life of debauchery, in March 1547. One of his nobles wrote that 'women rather than years killed him.'[11] Henri II ascended the throne with Catherine as his queen. The Huguenots hoped that the new king would be more sympathetic to them. At the start of his reign he was prepared to be more tolerant than his father, but was curious to know more about their beliefs. Thus, he requested one of the heretics be brought to him so that he could question the man about his faith.

A humble tailor was chosen in the hope that he would be awestruck and tongue-tied when in the presence of the king and his aristocratic entourage. Yet, he was neither of these and spoke passionately and movingly about his faith and genuine beliefs. His courageous answers astonished and alarmed Diane, who loathed Protestants. Worried that Henri might be swayed by the tailor's answers, she did her best to torment the poor man. 'In Protestant eyes she was the very incarnation of pagan immorality.'[12] They thought of her as a sinner for committing adultery with the king. Unfortunately, the tailor responded fervently, 'Madame, rest satisfied with having corrupted France, and do not mingle your filth with a thing so sacred as the Truth of God.'[13] Henri was furious that he dared to speak to his mistress in this way and ordered him to be immediately burned at the stake.

The king, queen, Diane, and courtiers watched from a window of the *Hôtel* des Tournelles in Paris as the heroic Huguenot took almost thirty minutes to die. Instead of screaming in agony, the man fixed his eyes on Henri and did not flinch until he lost consciousness. Although Henri found the tailor's bravery profoundly unsettling and vowed never to watch another man burn, he pursued a rigid policy of oppression towards Huguenots throughout his reign. He encouraged his subjects to unite in a crusade against them, but most Catholics were horrified by the treatment meted out to Protestants. They wanted a peaceful life with all religions living harmoniously.

In defiance of continued persecution, not only from Catholics in high places but from threatening, ragged, poverty-stricken mobs from the slums, Huguenots began fighting back. In a frenzy of iconoclastic violence they mutilated priceless statues and icons, including an important statue of the Virgin Mary with the infant Jesus in her arms.

Long after my ancestors left the parish of Saint-Éloi, it became a filthy slum. Many Huguenots lived alongside the desperately poor Catholics, who violated them at the slightest provocation. Huguenots, although equally impoverished, were on the whole industrious and proud, whereas the Catholics in this area tended to be full of animosity towards them on account of their faith. Dressed in rags, and full of hatred, they formed dangerous gangs who roamed the city streets. Protestants and Catholics alike were constantly hungry, and usually encumbered by hordes of children who were lucky to survive the squalor in which they lived.

It was normal for women to have as many as fourteen children, but many died in infancy and few grew to adulthood. There was no legal age for marriage, and life expectancy was short. Horrendous childbirth practices and lack of hygiene killed many women before the age of thirty. Diseases such as smallpox, scarlet fever, and tuberculosis were common and usually ended in death or deformity. The urban poor were hardest hit, but no family was left unaffected.

Huguenots living in Saint-Éloi and other similar places were almost blindingly devout and resolute, which was rather injudicious of them as they and their children were at constant risk of assault. Not being as brave as my ancestors, I am certain that had I been in their unfortunate position I would rapidly have converted. The wealthier folk were also in great danger every time they stepped out into the dark, narrow streets, as vandals were often lurking in the shadows ready to slit the throat of a detested Huguenot, especially a rich one.

Over the years Henri continued with his father's interests in the arts, war, and the persecution of Protestants. He was determined to suppress the Reformation and became even more ruthless than François had been. Concerned that so many nobles had converted, he issued the Edict of Châteaubriant in 1551. It stated that courts were to severely step-up abusing heretics. All Protestant 'vermin'[14] must be eliminated from the realm. Henri set up a burning chamber into which men, women, children, and infants were thrown and burned alive in full view of the public, while the beating of drums silenced their screams and the final utterances of their faith. He encouraged Catholics to watch them suffer, but most were astonished and humbled at how bravely the early converts accepted their cruel fate. They were true martyrs who counted it a privilege to die for Christ in this way.

Hardly a week passed by without them being cruelly tortured, burned, drowned, or beheaded, not for thieving or killing, but simply because they chose to follow a faith of their choice. They were forbidden to worship or to mention their religion, even in their own homes. If heard uttering heresies they had their tongues cut out, or worse. Every opportunity to humiliate them was enthusiastically taken. Huguenots were completely taken aback at the outrage and hatred caused by their conversion, and sympathetic Catholics were powerless to do anything about it. One inevitably thinks of the similarity between the treatment of the Huguenots in the sixteenth and seventeenth centuries, and the way the Jews were treated under the Nazis in the twentieth century – inhumanity caused by religion never seems to end.

Although a relatively small percentage of the population had followed Calvin at this stage, it included some important members of the aristocracy, notably, Louis, Prince de Condé, and his older brother, the first prince of the blood, Antoine de Bourbon and his wife, Jeanne d'Albret, daughter of François's sister, Marguerite. Antoine was weak-willed and not as devout as Jeanne and his brother. Over the years he wavered between the two religions depending on which was most popular at court or the stronger in battle, earning the sobriquet *ondoyant* – one whose mind changes. Being the elder son, he was head of the House of Bourbon who were loyal to the king, and rivals of the powerful House of Guise. Despite his weak demeanour, Antoine was better-looking than his shorter, pockmarked, but far more courageous and charismatic younger brother, the Prince de Condé.

By the middle of the sixteenth century the realm was floundering from inflation due to the endless foreign wars and rising prices, largely as a result of the influx of silver from the New World. The king was desperate for France to become more dominant in Europe and pursued numerous unsuccessful battles with Spain over Italy. The emperor, Charles V, abdicated in 1556 and his son Philip II inherited the Spanish crown. Henri was eventually forced to renounce any further claims and signed the contentious Treaty of Cateau-Cambrésis on 3 April 1559 with Queen Elizabeth and a day later with Philip. This finally brought an end to the ruinous series of wars between France and Spain for the control of Italy, leaving Habsburg Spain in the ascendancy.

Many felt that they had been betrayed by the stroke of a kingly pen, and Catherine was devastated when her hopes of recovering her lost patrimony were dashed. However, she gained some solace from the betrothal of their eldest daughter Elisabeth to Philip, the powerful king of Spain, which partly sealed the agreement. His first marriage was to Mary I, who had died the previous year. She is known as 'Bloody Mary' for her merciless attempt to reverse the religion of England to Catholicism, and for burning Protestants.

To celebrate the marriage by proxy of Elisabeth and Philip and the signing of the Treaty of Cateau-Cambrésis, a jousting tournament was held near Place des Vosges in Paris at the end of June. It was watched by Catherine and Diane as well as ladies and gentlemen of the court. On the third day the king challenged Gabriel, Compte de Montgomery, captain of his Scottish guard, to break a lance. It started well but much to the horror of the spectators, Henri was fatally injured and died of sepsis ten days later, aged forty, at *Hôtel* des Tournelles. He left the frail and sickly fifteen-year-old François II to the mercies of his unpopular mother, who upon her husband's death was thrown into the machinations of the vicious and corrupt world of court politics.

CHAPTER FIVE

'The Daughter Of Merchants'

But when a ruler occupies a state in an area that has a different language, different customs and different institutions, then things get tough.[1]

Niccolò Machiavelli, *The Prince*

Catherine was left distraught and frightened after the death of Henri and grieved for months in her private chambers, the walls of which were covered in black silk. Rather than wearing white, the preferred colour of mourning among European queens, she wore mainly black and a small collar of ermine – a symbol of royalty – for many years. Her youngest daughter Marguerite de Valois mentioned in her *mémoires* that on the previous night her mother had 'dreamed that she saw him wounded in the eye, as it really happened.'[2] Catherine had an abiding belief in seers and astrology, as well as in her own ability to predict the future.

She became a committed follower and admirer of Nostradamus, and his influence later affected many of the decisions she made regarding the future of the realm and her children. Nostradamus was a physician and soothsayer who even today, nearly five centuries later, evokes an air of mystery and awe and is accredited with correctly predicting many major world events. He was born Michel de Nostredame in a small town in Provence, but later Latinised his name.

When young he attended a university in Avignon but was unable to attain his degree, as the university was forced to close due to an outbreak of plague. This seemed to inspire him as he started researching herbal remedies before setting himself up as a professional healer. He believed that some of his concoctions could help avert this terrible disease. But there was no cure or prevention, and he lost his first wife and two children to the Black Death. He was later accused of heresy and in order to avoid standing trial, and the wrath of the church, he spent the next decade as an apothecary travelling through Italy and France. He eventually settled in the small town of Salon-de-Provence with his new wife and their six children.

In later life, Nostradamus moved away from medicine and began to take an interest in the occult and almanacs – the horoscopes of the sixteenth century. He started printing pamphlets, which included notices of future events and detailed astrological predictions. Feeling vulnerable on religious grounds, he devised a method of obscuring his messages by writing prophecies in the form of quatrains – clever four-line poems written in a mixture of French, Italian, Greek, and Latin. They were deliberately enigmatic to lessen his chances of being prosecuted for dabbling in mystical practices.

Each poem had to be deciphered by his clientele to establish the exact nature of the prediction. Nostradamus and the quatrains received a mixed reaction. Some thought him evil, a fake, or insane but many, especially the elite and the nobility, were enthralled and started requesting horoscopes and psychic advice from him. In 1555 his book *Les Prophéties* was published and has rarely been out of print.

In an age of arranged marriages, wives, especially royal wives, could not expect their husbands to be faithful, but Henri's long devotion to Diane was different. Catherine was forced to bury her resentment of her husband's paramour while he was alive. She had learnt to wear a mask of friendship when faced with anyone who was a threat to her or the kingdom – it was a useful tool. She also had a habit of calling people she distrusted or disliked 'my friend.'[3] Her husband's mistress definitely fell into this category. Immediately after Henri died, Diane was sent into exile and granted the Château de Chaumont but she preferred her own Château d'Anet, and lived there in isolated comfort for the rest of her life while continually making trouble for the Huguenots behind the scenes. She was ordered to return all the gifts Henri had bestowed upon her over the years, including items comprising the crown jewels and her beloved home the beautiful Château de Chenonceau; one of the most desirable properties in the country. After removing all traces of her rival, Catherine quickly made this impressive château in the Loire Valley one of her favoured residences in which to hold the spectacular and lavish entertainments for which she became acclaimed. She spent a fortune improving and expanding the building, even extending the Grand Gallery along the existing bridge to cross the River Cher.

Henri's death left a power void which had far-reaching effects. The heavy, ancient, bejewelled Crown of Charlemagne was placed on François's fifteen-year-old head in September 1559 at Rheims by Charles, Cardinal de Lorraine, but the mastery of ruling was far from lying in his feeble grasp. François was also king consort of Scotland having married his childhood friend, the statuesque, golden-haired, confident sixteen-year-old Mary, Queen of Scots the year before while still the dauphin. Her uncles, the urbane and eloquent François Duc de Guise, known as *le Balafré* – the Scarface, due to a scar received in battle – and his brother, the influential, cunning, silver-tongued Cardinal de Lorraine were the main instigators in arranging the betrothal, and her escape from her troublesome Scottish realm at the age of five.

Taking advantage of their relationship to Mary, the brothers speedily filled the void. The duke, who was fearless and authoritative in battle, took charge of all military campaigns and the cardinal attended to foreign, domestic, and financial affairs. 'For the Guises, it was a chance in a thousand. Their dreams were realised. At a stroke they were regents of the kingdom'[4] in all but name.

They moved into the Louvre with the young couple and their courtiers the day Henri died, insidiously taking over the reins of governing the realm in what can only be described as a *coup d'état*. Within days of the king's accession the English ambassador, Nicholas Throckmorton, remarked that 'the house of Guise ruleth and doth all about the French King.'[5] Referring to the cardinal, a Venetian statesman commented, 'He is not well beloved. He is insincere, and has a nature both artful and avaricious, equally in his own affairs as in those of the King.'[6] In an age when physical courage was prized above all, although the cardinal was feared, unlike his brother, deep down he was a coward.

Catherine, now the queen mother, was shocked at this sudden move by the Guises whom she disliked intensely, as she had never forgotten how badly they and their family had treated her in the past. She had no alternative but to outwardly accept the situation, assume a restrained demeanour, and wear her mask of friendship while surreptitiously advising her son.

The young king was determined to show these interlopers and their partisans that he held his mother in high esteem. In an attempt to stress her importance to him he opened all official acts with words, 'This being the good pleasure of my Lady-Mother and I also approving of every opinion that she holdeth, am content and command that...'[7] The Guises, in their presumptuous supremacy, underestimated Catherine and continued to make no attempt to hide their dislike of the 'Florentine shopkeeper,'[8] as she became known among the courtiers. Mary, Queen of Scots is famously said to have once referred to her mother-in-law as '*Cette fille de marchands*'[9] – the daughter of merchants. 'So vulgar a prejudice no longer had any sanction at the French Court, where everyone was in pursuit of fortune and the only distinction between titled traders and the others was that the aristocrat obtained by birth what the bourgeois had yet to acquire.'[10]

The House of Guise was highly unpopular with many of the nobility. In the past kings had ruled in an uneasy entente with the ambitious, interfering nobles but now Guise power was absolute. Their domination threatened the Catholic House of Montmorency – an ancient line of powerful nobles – and the Bourbon brothers Antoine de Bourbon and Louis de Bourbon, Prince de Condé. These dynastic tensions were interwoven with religious and social concerns. Condé, Jeanne d'Albret and Antoine, now king and queen of the small principality of Navarre after the death of Jeanne's father, followed Calvin whereas Anne – pronounced Annay – de Montmorency and his immediate family were Catholic. But Anne's nephews – Admiral Gaspard de Coligny and his brothers Ôdet, Cardinal de Châtillon, and François d'Andelot all became leading Huguenots.

Montmorency had been an influential and close advisor to François I and Henri II and had held the coveted title of Great Constable of France, the most senior position in the military hierarchy. However, he was not an admirer of the queen mother and formed an alliance with Jaques d'Albon, Seigneur de Saint-André and the Duc de Guise. They identified themselves as defenders of the Catholic faith in what became known as the Triumvirate.* Apart from Paris and the immediate outskirts, their administration was considered untenable throughout Protestant Europe. Persecution by burning or beheading of Protestants continued relentlessly for the duration of their fanatical rule.

Their aim was to save the kingdom from Protestantism and to covertly dislodge Catherine from her position of supremacy. She was in an impossible position as the Triumvirate and the extremist Catholics were backed by the pope and Philip of Spain, but the Huguenots Antoine and Condé were next in line to the throne, should all her sons die without an heir. Consequently, to ensure the safety of the Valois rule she spent the rest of her life trying to appease whichever faction was in the ascendant.

The queen mother is widely thought to have been a devotee of Machiavelli and his book *The Prince*, dedicated to her father. She

---

*   Triumvirate - three men holding power.

certainly followed many of his harsh principles. Machiavelli believed that to earn the respect of his subjects, a ruler must be prepared to punish or eliminate those who endanger the good of the realm. Hence, his name became synonymous with scheming and authoritarianism.

In the all-important classification of lineage, the Bourbon brothers had the rights of guidance over François. Their main aim was to save the king from the malevolent influence of the commandeering Guises; therefore, they believed that it was necessary to remove them by force. This led to Throckmorton suggesting to Queen Elizabeth that it was time to overthrow the hated brothers and help the Protestants. 'Now is the time to spend money and it will never be better spent.'[11] She grudgingly agreed, and sacks of gold and silver were secretly sent to France.

In early 1560 a contingent of conspirators including Charles de Castelnau and Condé, arguably the silent instigator of the plot, conceived a daring plan to overthrow the Guises by force and liberate the king. A minor nobleman and adventurer, Jean du Barry, was used as a scapegoat and left to organise and lead the troops. They consisted mainly of inexperienced Scottish mercenaries and former loyal royal soldiers, who were dissatisfied with their treatment under the Guise regime. The antagonists planned the attack to take place at Château de Blois where the court were assembled, but spies abounded and the cowardly cardinal soon discovered the intrigue and was filled with terror, especially when he heard that the Protestants had the backing of the queen of England.

Thinking that he had outwitted the adversaries, the cardinal moved the court from Blois to the safer, fortified Château d'Amboise, but the Huguenots also had spies and quickly learnt of the change. As expected, a band of assailants armed with pitchforks, daggers, and butchers' knives besieged Château d'Amboise but were captured by the king's soldiers, who had been forewarned and were waiting for them. This collusion was so badly organised that it was doomed from the start.

The odious Duc de Guise who 'revelled in the very orgy of blood,'[12] ordered Jean du Barry to be hung, drawn, and quartered. The remains of his body were displayed on the gates of the town as a lesson for the townspeople not to dabble in heresies. Hundreds of suspected Huguenot plotters were put to death. Commoners were burned and nobles were put on trial and beheaded, regardless of whether they were guilty or not. At Amboise people fought for a space, perching precariously on rooftops, branches of trees, or window ledges, all hoping for a good view of the beheadings. The horror was increased when the entire court gathered excitedly at the château windows after dinner to observe the decapitation of the aristocratic Protestants, whose grisly heads were later paraded around the town on pikes.

As one nobleman mounted the scaffold, he bent down and dipped his hands in the blood of his companions, and raising them to Heaven cried out, 'Oh God Most Good and Most Gracious, behold the innocent blood of those who belong to You, whose death You will not leave unpunished.'[13] Not everyone enjoyed watching the despicable treatment of Huguenot nobles and many, who privately sympathised with them, were repulsed at the sight. 'I am astonished that the King is counselled to put so many honest lords and gentlemen to death'[14] admonished Condé, sickened by the carnage.

After the massacre Théodore-Agrippa d'Aubigné, a soldier, chronicler, and interpreter of Huguenotism, remembered as a ten-year-old child walking through the bustling throng of Amboise with his father. Suddenly they came upon the withering heads of some eminent nobles fixed on spikes above the gates where, in keeping with tradition, they had been placed to moulder. 'They have slaughtered France, the butchers!'[15] cried his father. In excess of one thousand Huguenots were hanged or burned to death during this episode, which was later dubbed the Amboise Conspiracy.

The atrocities continued for weeks, with rotting bodies left hanging from hooks on the battlements of the château. 'Ten, twenty, fifty, were thrown in sacks into the Loire. In so far as mercy was shown, it was by sparing some from the galleys.'[16] The notorious slave galleys were the most dreaded of all punitive measures. Each galley held up to three hundred men, who were tethered together and chained securely to their oars. Their sentences varied from five years, to life, it made no difference. Fastened by the neck with thick chains weighing 150 pounds, they were made to row the rough seas until most died of exhaustion and hunger.

The first stirrings of the French Wars of Religion had begun, dominating François's brief reign. Condé was arrested in late October on suspicion of organising the conspiracy, although he had been with the king at Amboise at the time. He was later released, probably due to the intervention of François. Hatred for the Guises increased among Protestants throughout Europe after the killings. 'So extreme is the hatred revealed by the nobility and people against these gentlemen,' exclaimed Julio Alvarotto, the Ferraran ambassador, 'that it is impossible to express it in writing.'[17]

Catherine adored her children, especially her good-looking third son Henri d'Anjou, whom she lovingly called *Chers Yeux* – Dear Eyes. 'Her son became the god of her idolatry, at the shrine of whose will she sacrificed everything,'[18] Marguerite wrote of her brother. The royal children were brought up in the splendour of a glittering court life, moving from one magnificent château to another including Blois, Amboise, Fontainebleau, Saint-Maur, Chambord, Montceaux, Chenonceau, and Château de Saint-Germain-en-Laye. They never stayed long in any of them but moved from one to the other looking for fresh game to hunt, and to avoid the stench and risk of disease caused by the lack of sanitation. The entire court including priceless furniture, fine tapestries from Brussels, gold and silver plate, and horses for hunting and jousting moved with them. As was customary, the rooms of the châteaux were often only furnished for the duration of the king's visit.

All the queen mother desired was to protect her children, the king, the Valois dynasty, and of course herself, at any cost. Although Catholic, as were the vast majority of the population, regardless of Admiral de Coligny being a Huguenot, she admired him and listened to his advice. She knew that he was faithful to the royal family but was undecided whether some of the more militant Huguenots were plotting against the king, as the Guises maintained, or if they themselves were responsible for the growing unrest and bloodshed. She was only too aware that they wanted to dispose of her, but felt that she could trust the Bourbon brothers, Coligny, and their advocates. As usual, she was hedging her bets.

On Coligny's recommendation, Catherine started seeking advice from her chancellor, Michel de l'Hôpital, who, although Catholic, was sympathetic to the Huguenots and continually strove for peace. He believed that the majority including my ancestors supported the king and wished to live peacefully, but the extremists were politically motivated and determined to cause trouble. In the hope of reaching a compromise the chancellor proposed a meeting between the hierarchy of both Protestants and Catholics. The plan was universally supported by moderates on both sides but was opposed by the pope.

The conciliation policy was intended to ease tensions, but had the opposite effect and killings, looting, and unrest spread throughout the kingdom. 'So far Huguenots had lurked in dark places and cried from dungeons. On rare occasions when they had struck back, it was done under the cloak of conspiracy, and despair. With the assembly at Fontainebleau it changed its attitude.'[19] Opposed to burning innocent people they counteracted by destroying prized holy artefacts and priests' vestments.

'When the Admiral claimed that his petition could be signed by fifty thousand souls, the thought lay behind: could be supported by fifty thousand swords! In a word they had the power, and, if need be, the will to resist.'[20] This was a warning to the Guises and their advocates that the Huguenots had the manpower to defend themselves if necessary. They responded with counter-threats.

Using her diplomatic skills, with the support of l'Hôpital and Coligny, Catherine enthusiastically immersed herself in organising the assembly, which was to be held at Fontainebleau in August. Much as she disliked the Guises and wished to be free of them, she had to tread carefully as the realm needed their military strength, and they had a large and powerful following. The cardinal, dressed in red robes and wearing a heavy gold chain and pectoral cross, adorned by a large ruby, and the much-feared duke grudgingly agreed to attend.

Unbeknown to Catherine, the cardinal had been forewarned that Antoine and Condé were planning to capture Lyon. Thus, they surreptitiously planned to use this opportunity to lure them from their territory in the south to the assembly and charge them with treason. The Bourbon brothers suspected a conspiracy, and to the queen mother's annoyance refused to attend. The meeting continued as planned without the Huguenot leaders, but it was doomed from the start by the ongoing rivalry between the Guises and the Bourbons. 'The assembly of Fontainebleau thus prepared the way for conflict, and in doing so influenced the future history of France.'[21]

The Guises eventually succeeded in implicating Antoine and Condé as leading conspirators in the Huguenot revolt, which took place as expected. Because they had spent their childhood at court and were cousins of the king they were given a stay of execution, but Condé was imprisoned at Amboise pending trial. His ineffectual and spineless elder brother managed to avoid the same fate by persuading François that he was innocent. The exasperated cardinal, aware that both brothers were responsible, grumbled in disgust that Antoine de Bourbon 'is the most cowardly soul there ever was!'[22] The duplicitous queen mother, who cried at the drop of a hat, sobbed her heart out when Condé was imprisoned. She needed him, and his loyalty to her family, and did not want to see him beheaded, but after visiting him at Amboise she wrote:

> I have [come] this morning from my journey to Amboise where I have been visiting a little gallant [the Prince de Condé], who has nothing in his brain but war and tempest. I assure you that whoever finds himself there will not get out again without leave, for the place is already strong and I have been adding to the fortifications. I have also had a good many doors and windows walled up and have had strong iron grating put to others.[23]

Condé was duly tried and condemned to death on the charge of *lèse-majesté* with the execution date set for 10 December, but the wheel of fortune was in his favour. While out hunting on a freezing day in November the king caught a chill, which developed into an ear infection and his life hung in the balance. According to tradition and the Estates General, if the king died it was beyond dispute that Antoine, being the first prince of the blood, was the legitimate regent for the ten-year-old dauphin, Charles, and would free his brother. The king's death would also help the Huguenots because the Guises would lose much of their authority. Their niece Mary, Queen of Scots would no longer be queen consort of France, and their power considerably diminished. They, of course, prayed that the king would live.

The queen mother, however, had other ideas as she coveted the regency for herself. She was aware that if Antoine became regent she could be banished, and her young son brought up under the influence of the Protestant House of Bourbon. Even worse, as Antoine was so unsure of his faith, Charles could fall into the hands of the dreaded Guises. Thus, she wasted no time in persuading him to surrender his legal claim to the regency. She reminded him that his brother was due to be executed in five days and, as he was still under suspicion of treason, he could be accused of sedition and suffer the same fate. He would lose his protector if François died. Among other incentives, she agreed to drop the charges against him and to release Condé from prison. Fearful of being imprisoned and condemned to die with his brother, Antoine agreed to sign a document ceding his right to the regency to Catherine.

CHAPTER SIX

◇━━◇━━━◇━━◇

'The Black Queen'

Since a ruler has to be able to act the beast, he should take on the traits of the fox and the lion; the lion can't defend itself against the snares and the fox can't defend itself from wolves.[1]

Niccolò Machiavelli, The Prince

After only eleven months on the throne, François died on 5 December 1560 – Nostradamus had predicted that Catherine's eldest son would die before he was eighteen. Her second son, a frail ten-year-old boy who was prone to ill health, was immediately declared Charles IX.

The death of the king and the queen mother's regency created huge problems for the Guises, who until then had total control of running the country. Many also objected to a mere woman being in such a powerful position, as this was a time when females were deemed inferior. Her final promise to Antoine had been to award him the title of lieutenant general, which was currently held by the Duc de Guise. He was enraged and loath to relinquish such an important position, let alone to a Huguenot who in his opinion might use his considerable authority to wage war against him. He complained to his ally Philip of Spain about the means the queen mother had used to influence Antoine, forcing her to write to her daughter Elisabeth in the hope that she would use her influence with her husband to defend her:

> *I want to tell you plainly what is the truth that all this trouble has been for no other cause except for the hate which this entire realm has for the Cardinal of Lorraine and the Duke of Guise… you know how they treated me during the time of the late King, your brother… if they had been able to do it, they would have appointed themselves to power and would have left me to one side. I want to tell you all this in detail in order that if, for the purpose of strengthening themselves by the support of the King, your husband, they send something secretly to make him believe that they have been put out of power because of religion… you can tell them the truth.[2]*

Catherine's cunning move was a huge political achievement, as by securing the regency she now had the power to prevent the belligerent nobles from tearing the country apart, and to safeguard the kingdom for her sons. She insisted on sleeping in Charles's bedchamber and keeping him at her side at all times to ensure that no one, particularly the Guise faction, were able to gain access to him. Meanwhile, the newly widowed Mary, Queen of Scots's *raison d'être* was in tatters and she became redundant. Catherine immediately demanded that she return the crown jewels and proceeded to treat Mary much as she had her rival Diane de Poitiers; wearing her mask of friendship, behaving as a loving mother-in-law, but secretly planning to send her as far away as possible.

The eleven-year-old Charles, dressed in a black velvet doublet embroidered with gold lace, and black feathered hat, out of respect for the death of his brother François, was crowned at Rheims on 15 May 1561. He wept throughout his coronation and as the massive crown was laid on his diminutive head, he cried out in distress that it was 'too heavy.'[3] Not a good omen. His mother continued to preside over his council and control state affairs, but she never had total authority as in many parts of the country the nobility held more power than the monarch. Before any decision could be enforced, she needed the backing of the nobles as well as the king's seal of approval, even though he was only eleven years old. Religious unrest was at its height by the summer of that year prompting Calvin to write to Théodore de Bèze, his trusted disciple in France, 'In twenty cities, or about that number, the godly [Huguenots] have been slaughtered by raging mobs. In only one has there been judicial action by magistrates.'[4]

Determined to find a solution to alleviate the religious conflict, regardless of opposition from the pope, Catherine decided that her best option was to summon church leaders from both sides to yet another conference. Accordingly, in July of that year, a national council of Protestant and Catholic clergy gathered at the refectory in the Dominican convent in Poissy on the banks of the River Seine, about fifteen miles northwest of Paris. The proceedings were opened with a speech given by the chancellor. Huguenots were represented by Bèze; an intelligent and sophisticated nobleman known for his tact and sensitivity. The Cardinal de Lorraine was spokesman for the Catholics.

After a cordial discussion it looked as if the cardinal and Bèze, who had not met before, were about to reach an agreement with the former conceding, 'I adjure you to confer with me; you will find that I am not as black as I am painted.'[5] When it came to the matter of the observance of Mass, Bèze, his acclaimed tact deserting him, announced, 'We say that His [Christ's] body is as far removed from bread and wine as the highest heaven is from earth.'[6] A horrified silence was followed by the outraged Catholic clergy shouting in fury at his blasphemous words. Regardless, they continued to discuss the situation for a few more days but failed to agree, leaving the queen mother's aspirations for a compromise in tatters. This abortive conference is known as the Colloquy of Poissy, which did nothing other than to incite deeper division between the two religions.

Soon after the requisite period of mourning for her eldest son had passed, Catherine reinstated a replica of her revered father-in-law's *La Petite Bande*. She surrounded herself with beautiful, beguiling young ladies known as *L'Escadron Volant* – The Flying Squadron. These overtly seductive, aristocratic *femmes fatales* were dressed like goddesses in white and silver silk gowns. Their lives revolved purely around court life with its immorality, jealousies, competitiveness, and spitefulness. The formation of this band of beauties was a surprising departure from the queen mother's moralistic persona, but she had a hidden agenda.

The girls were encouraged to charm the contentious nobles, both Huguenot and Catholic. She also used them to spy on her enemies as a means of securing power, and, if beneficial, to sleep with them. Brantôme, the court chronicler, who lived at court for a time and idolised Catherine, wrote, 'I do not greatly value them, but I should dream over them and amuse myself too much. Beauty abounded, all majesty, all charm, all grace; happy was he who could touch with love such ladies… ladies and demoiselles who were beautiful, agreeable, very accomplished, and well sufficient to set fire to the whole world. Indeed, in their best days, they burned up a good part of it, as much us gentlemen of the Court as others who approached the flame.'[7]

Apart from tempting her enemies with her alluring maidens, Catherine distracted the nobility from incendiary actions by providing them with endless entertainment. Charles's court became a hotbed of intrigue with indiscriminate lovemaking, nudity, and riotous drinking parties lasting all night, but Catherine remained upright and respectable. She was popular with those who were close to her but never gained the trust of the people, especially in Paris and the surrounding areas. 'In the eyes of the great and powerful she remained the Florentine shopkeeper; to the people she was simply "the Italian". Her origin was the Queen Mother's greatest weakness.'[8] She was laughed at for her habit of shedding tears whenever it proved difficult for her to get her own way. She wept a lot 'for her children, for France, and for herself.'[9]

Protestantism was attracting many of the most illustrious, influential, and aristocratic nobles in the land. Most were genuine, but others converted as much for political as religious reasons, or because it was fashionable. Hence, the New Religion slowly began to gain a degree of influence over the royal family, and Huguenotism became *de rigueur.* The time for reflection came later.

Huguenots were now openly accepted at court. Condé carried out his preaching in his rooms, not far from the king, and Coligny was admitted to the royal council. He also spent much time advising the young king, who became so fond of him that he called him *'Mon Père'.*[10] Ôdet, Cardinal de Châtillon, Coligny's brother, nearly lost his life when he rescued a Protestant preacher from a Catholic mob, who were about to murder him, and took him to the safety of his house. The mobs later stormed the house, and the preacher was dragged out and burned in the marketplace. It was only by hiding that Ôdet was able to escape the same fate.

Fervent Catholics were extremely concerned about the growing popularity of Protestants at court. The Spanish ambassador, Perrenot de Chantonnay, who was particularly disturbed about the acceptance of Coligny and his brothers, reported that 'the Cardinal de Châtillon, the Admiral, and François d'Andelot are continually at the palace. When once the gates are open, the King and Queen Mother are never without them. Already this has attracted attention and raised a fear that little by little they may spread the opinions with which they are generally said to be affected.'[11]

Coligny was highly respected and regarded among the Huguenots as their saviour. Referring to him, Calvin wrote, 'There is one among the chiefs who acts wisely.'[12] But a Catholic courtier caustically grumbled, 'They [Huguenots] speak of God as though He had revealed to them His most high secrets. They do nothing but sing psalms, translated by Marot and Bèze into the French tongue, small in size and set to music. When ladies find themselves together, they hold a concert and sing the said psalms, the stable-lacqueys doing the same.'[13]

At this stage the queen mother and Jeanne d'Albret were still friendly, regardless of Jeanne's committed allegiance to the Huguenots. Catherine, who was not particularly devout, was prepared to accept her friend's beliefs provided she promised not to cause trouble. Emulating her late father-in-law's philosophy, she divided the Huguenots into two groups – peaceful and loyal, and evil and troublesome – but she was in a difficult position and did not know which way to turn. She preferred her loyal Protestant friends to the pompous Guise brothers and their supporters, as she knew that they and the Bourbons desired her to remain in power, whereas the Guise faction were desperate to depose her. But she could not afford to fall out with them yet.

Although ostensibly on the side of orthodoxy, Catherine was bewildered by the conversion of so many of the nobility, and for a time was tempted to follow their lead. It was widely accepted that she was friendly with many of the Huguenot leaders, and that the royal children were being brought up as Protestants. Henri d'Anjou – later Henri III – was so captivated with the religion that he insisted on singing psalms and reading bibles in French rather than Latin. He is known to have thrown his sister Marguerite's Book of Hours into the fire and threatened that their mother would have her whipped if she refused to convert. Much later Anjou, who as a child is said to have called himself the 'Little Huguenot', became a zealous Catholic and took an active role fighting against them in the Religious Wars.

Marguerite was the only sibling who, with the support of her lady of the bedchamber, Madame de Curton, refused to contemplate sacrificing her strong Catholic faith. She later wrote that 'the whole Court was infected with heresy about the time of the conference of Poissy. It was with great difficulty that I resisted and preserved myself from the change of religion at that time. Many ladies and lords belonging to the Court strove to convert me to Huguenotism.'[14] The courtiers were now bitterly divided between the two religions.

It was also common knowledge that Catherine had invited Bèze to remain at court, where he was sanctioned to preach to the many aristocratic converts. The Guises were so concerned that they attempted to kidnap Catherine's favourite son Anjou to save him from his heretic family. The ten-year-old boy was approached several times by various members of the Guise family who insisted that he would be happier if he lived with his elder sister Claude, who was an ardent Catholic. The roguish twelve-year-old son of the Duc de Guise, also called Henri, who had been brought up with the royal children since infancy, instructed, 'You will be carried off at midnight and passed out of a window near the gate of the park, and then you will be placed in a coach, and be in Lorraine before anyone knows that you are gone.'[15] Intimidated by the older boy, and terrified at the thought of being passed through a window and kidnapped, Anjou informed his mother, who was horrified. The Guises refuted the whole episode, leaving Catherine with no choice other than to let the matter drop; but her hatred and fear of them intensified.

The queen mother condoned and seemingly encouraged Protestants at court, but she had a difficult decision to make as the problems facing the monarchy were extremely complex and the country was on the brink of civil war. Ever aware that the vast majority of the country was Catholic, but also of the power the Huguenots now held, she had to tread cautiously. It was technically illegal to practise Protestantism, but as so many prominent nobles and members of the royal family had converted, something had to be done to protect their political standing.

After taking advice from her chancellor and Coligny, in her capacity as regent, she signed the Edict of January in 1562 while at Saint-Germain-en-Laye. This permitted Protestant synods and consistories, and Huguenots were allowed to establish places of worship in barns or caves in areas outside city walls where riots were less likely to arise. They were only allowed to hold services in these places during daylight hours, and not on Sundays or Catholic feast days. Preference was, as always, given to nobles who were granted the privilege to practise their religion on their estates. The edict also stated that compensation must be made for any Catholic property or items that had been stolen or destroyed by Huguenots during the previous years of unrest.

Fanatical Catholics were furious. They were concerned that Huguenots would start meeting in public areas, reading the Bible in French, and preaching heresies. As usual, Catherine's Machiavellian strategy was to play one religion against the other. She explained to the Protestants that the king was determined to make all his subjects 'clearly understand his intention to enforce this Edict that nobody can be able to allege any pretext nor occasion to break it.'[16] To prove her orthodoxy and keep the Catholics happy, she told them that the edict was only an temporary measure that the king was forced to take to keep the Huguenots from causing more problems.

Jeanne d'Albret decided that she needed a break from court life and from her husband. Antoine's fondness for other women and his ambivalence towards his faith had taken its toll, and, although their marriage had initially been happy, they resolved to separate. Disappointed with the edict and repulsed by the recent atrocities meted out to the Huguenots, Jeanne decided to flee. She travelled with her suite and their two-year-old daughter, Catherine, named after the queen mother, to seek refuge in her principality of Béarn, reluctantly leaving behind their beloved young son, Henri de Bourbon. Catherine insisted on keeping him at court as she felt it gave her some control over his 'activist' mother. Jeanne was unwell and was forced to stop several times during the journey. Regardless of her husband's threat to have her imprisoned if she set foot in Vendôme, the ancestral seat of his family, she and her entourage interrupted their journey to stay at his château, although it was not safe to remain for more than a few days.

While resting there, Huguenot rioters stormed the town and ransacked Catholic churches including the ducal chapel, which housed the tombs of Antoine's ancestors. He was furious and blamed Jeanne. He threatened to arrest her and incarcerate her in a convent in Paris – the classic method of disposing of unwanted wives – but she was much shrewder than her husband and managed to escape before he was able to carry out his threat. Their marriage was now destroyed beyond repair.

At the age of twelve, Jeanne had been forced into a marrying William, Duke of Jülich-Cleves-Berg, brother of Anne of Cleves. She was a wilful child and had to be carried, kicking and screaming, to the altar by Anne de Montmorency. The marriage was annulled after four years.

Following in her mother Marguerite's footsteps, Jeanne eventually became the acknowledged spiritual and political leader of the Huguenots and worked tirelessly for equal rights for them until her death. She was also the prime mover behind many of the peace agreements. Much later she succumbed to encouraging the more militant converts to burn Catholic churches and destroy treasured holy relics in retaliation for the persecution they endured. She eventually advocated warfare, often accompanying the admiral and her brother-in-law the Prince de Condé to the battlefields to rally Huguenot forces.

Catherine de Médicis

CHAPTER SEVEN

The Beginning Of The End

So, if a leader does what it takes to win power and keep it,
his methods will always be reckoned honourable and highly
praised.[1]

Niccolò Machiavelli, *The Prince*

Following the Edict of January and Catherine's regency, the power of the House of Guise had diminished, and the family retreated to their vast estates in Champagne in the duchy of Lorraine. This was not only a great relief to the Huguenots, but also to increasingly Protestant Europe. However, their acquiescence was short-lived. On 1 March 1562, the Duc de Guise was travelling with his entourage of two hundred armed knights to attend Mass. As they passed through Vassy, they came across a gathering of Protestants innocently worshipping in a barn. Trumpets blaring, the knights began hurling rocks and shouting, 'Kill! Kill! By God's death, kill these Huguenots.'[2]

The congregants retaliated by throwing back whatever they could find. A rock hit the duke which was a grave offence as common folk were supposed to revere and respect the nobility. He was so irate that he immediately ordered his men to fortify the town and set fire to the modest barn. There was no escape and more than fifty unarmed men, women, and children were stabbed or burned to death, many while captive in the barn. Another two hundred were badly injured. The duke is said to have thought of this devastating bloodbath as nothing more than a regrettable incident. Parisians were elated and 'it made Guise the idol of all those who wanted to exterminate heresy.'[3] The taper was lit. It was just a question of when it would explode.

A month later, inflamed by monks and priests from Paris, Catholics massacred a group of Huguenots as they walked home happily singing psalms after holding a service in a barn in Sens. The massacre was even greater than that of Vassy. There were at least one hundred dead after they had been tortured, drowned, and raped, and their homes had been ransacked. These appalling incidents further fuelled the atmosphere of mistrust and fear that already existed and forced the Huguenots to retaliate.

As the royalists were otherwise engaged, being garrisoned along the Habsburg frontier, Coligny and Condé began seizing major towns. On 2 April, they and their men captured the important, walled city of Orléans where they raised the Huguenot standard. The latter promised to protect the Catholic inhabitants, but he was defenceless against the radical element, who wanted revenge.

> But it was not only with aristocrats and gentlemen that the Prince and Admiral had to deal. There was the rank and file of the party. And they soon found themselves powerless before its fanaticism. Condé had promised the Catholics in Orléans his protection, and they were left in possession of their churches, at least until 21st of April. Then the Huguenot zealots, goaded to fury by massacres at Sens, began their work of destruction. Church after church was either defaced or pillaged.[4]

Étienne Pasquier, a lawyer, *politique**, and chronicler wrote, 'Where the Huguenot is Master, he ruins the images and demolishes the

---

* *Politique* – a member of a moderate Catholic group.

sepulchres and tombs. On the other hand, the Catholic kills, murders, and drowns all those whom he knows to be of that sect, until the rivers overflow with them.'[5] The Huguenot rank and file did not need any encouragement and started savaging cherished icons and crosses in the Cathédrale Sainte-Croix in Orléans, causing the king's soldiers to grab their swords and charge to the scene, as uprisings spread throughout the kingdom causing untold atrocities. Several days later Huguenots seized Rouen, further enraging the Guises and their sycophants who began preparing for war, forcing the Huguenots to follow suit. This resulted in thirty years of uprisings and counter-offensives, largely stimulated by disputes between the aristocratic Houses. They were conducted in a haphazard and inconclusive manner, interspersed with spells of peace treaties and perilous truces.

Spies warned the Huguenot leaders that Guise was mustering a large army in Paris, and they began preparing to counter-attack. 'The more turbulent among the Huguenots seized their arms. Little bands of tens and twenties went galloping along the country roads, pressing on for the capital; Condé or the Admiral might have need of them.'[6] They did need these men and gathered together as many as possible from all walks of life. But they also urgently required help from friendly countries abroad for more fighting men and funds to arm themselves. Coligny was loath to ask for foreign help. 'He confessed that he would rather die than let the Huguenots first call in the stranger,'[7] but as most of the troops were in the hands of their enemy it was necessary to do so. Hence, numerous letters were dispatched to England, Switzerland, and Germany.

Queen Elizabeth, while sympathetic, was more interested in recovering Calais, which had been under English jurisdiction since taken by Edward III in 1347 but regained by the French in 1558. Nevertheless, she agreed to help but drove a hard bargain by demanding the town of Le Havre, known then as Le Havre-de-Grâce, and the return of Calais – her optimum goal – when the Huguenots had successfully won the war.

In accordance with the agreement, she sent three hundred of her troops to occupy Le Havre. This formed part of the unpopular and controversial Treaty of Hampton Court, which was eventually signed by Elizabeth and Condé in September 1562. The queen later declared, 'it was with good and sincere intentions towards the King our good brother that she occupied the Norman ports. It was merely a matter of saving the King of France's Protestant subjects from annihilation, and to procure for them by all good means, repose, peace, freedom, and deliverance from the said House of Guise or any adherents of the same.'[8]

The treaty did not go down well with many Catholics, the king, or with Catherine who constantly strove to establish a stable Anglo-French alliance. She had thought Elizabeth was her ally, but now began to view her as deceitful and untrustworthy for supporting the Huguenots. Furious, the queen mother wrote to her ambassador, 'To begin with I shall use all gentle means that are open to me and if they fail, I shall resolve myself to using hard and sharp ones in order to have the right of the matter.'[9]

Calvin, on hearing that the Protestants were planning to defend themselves against Guise and his army, warned, 'that if one drop of blood were shed, rivers would run with it throughout Europe.'[10] How true his words turned out to be.

With help from England and the German princes, money for weapons was raised and an army assembled. The national synod for the Reformed Church met in Paris and Huguenot leaders were officially elected. The ineffectual Antoine was universally considered the *chef muet* – the silent commander – followed by his far more dependable and fearless younger brother, Condé, but the true leader was the admiral; one of the country's most feared and respected warriors. Condé's religious adherence was genuine, but 'Antoine's connection with Huguenotism was a mere intrigue, crowned with betrayal. He was never sincerely a Protestant except in death.'[11]

Catherine, having alienated herself from the Guises, had no option but to put her trust in the Huguenot leaders, especially as Antoine was fighting on their side. She knew that she had many enemies at court as she had heard through her listening tube, cunningly concealed behind a tapestry in a council chamber, one of the Triumvirate Seigneur de Saint-André stating that in his opinion the queen mother should be stitched up in a sack and flung into the Seine. She was most relieved to hear Guise defend her and admonish Saint-André for even thinking of treating her in such a way. Concerned about her lack of popularity with the ultra-Catholics, she asked some of her trusted courtiers what the Parisians thought of her. They replied that 'the whole city was against her and that everybody called the chancellor a heretic.'[12] Surprised and shocked, she replied that her chancellor, Michel de l'Hôpital, was 'the best man in the world.'[13]

Terrified that she and the king might once again fall under Guise dominance, she wrote in confidence to Condé imploring him to 'save the children, the mother and the realm.'[14] At the same time, she wrote to Coligny begging him to seize Paris. On realising how potentially dangerous her words were, she ended, 'Burn this instantly,'[15] but he kept the letter; it could be useful one day. For their own protection, Coligny advised her to abandon court and flee with the king to the safety of Orléans, which was now the Huguenot stronghold.

She considered following his advice, but on hearing that Guise had persuaded the fickle Antoine to change allegiance and fight for them, she had no option but to remain at Fontainebleau. She knew that if the royal army emerged victorious the Estates General would endorse Antoine should he attempt to challenge her position as regent, and Catherine could be removed and possibly charged with treason.

Guise wasted no time in sending a formidable number of cavalrymen to capture the twelve-year-old Charles and his tearful mother, claiming to be concerned that the Huguenots were planning to take the royal family hostage. They refused to leave, but were forcibly removed and escorted to Paris, where they remained under house arrest. The duke and his brother had taken control of the government and the army, and Charles and his mother were once again at their mercy. As the king was held under 'protective custody' the Guise faction were *de facto* also in possession of the law, and Charles and Catherine were vulnerable and powerless. The queen mother had no option but to grovel. She denied having had any association with the Huguenots, or that she had ever condoned Protestantism, and that her friendship with the Huguenot leaders had all been a ploy. In the world of kings, princes, and courtiers, no one told the truth.

Catherine felt safer with the Huguenots, but with Antoine now fighting for the Catholics backed by Spain, and Paris providing them with numerous funds and a sizeable number of soldiers, she was aware that they had little chance of succeeding in battle. Predictably, she decided to curry favour with the Guises. She had no option.

Two months after the Massacre of Vassy, with the daunting prospect of fighting the royalists, now controlled by Guise and reinforced by a fearsome force of Spanish troops and Swiss mercenaries, the Huguenots prepared for battle. They were supported and funded by Elizabeth and the German princes, with Condé at the helm and the admiral second-in-command. The royalists were led by Montmorency with Guise as his deputy. It was the first time for over a century that two French armies had faced each other in battle, with family and friends fighting stoically and sorrowfully against each other. The Huguenots wore *surcoats* of white; the Bourbon colour of Condé, and the royalists wore royal purple. The Huguenots sang psalms while the Swiss mercenaries kissed the ground, as was their custom, and both sides waited nervously for the blast of trumpets giving them the signal to commence battle. Condé's strategy was to capture as many towns as possible in Normandy – Guise territory.

Although weaker in infantry, the Huguenots were more powerful in heavy cavalry. To begin with they were successful in seizing towns along the Loire and Rhône rivers, but their luck ran out when they attempted to hold Rouen, which was unfortunately besieged by the royalists in May 1562. The delighted queen mother arrived on horseback at Fort-Sainte-Catherine, above the city walls, to liaise with the royalists and watch from the ramparts as their men slaughtered the Huguenots. Apart from her desire to recapture this vitally important city, she was concerned that it might fall into the hands of the English.

Innocent inhabitants, both Huguenot and Catholic, were normally aware of an imminent attack and locked themselves in their houses, and prayed. If the Catholic army were attacking, Huguenot men young and old, student, artisan, peasant, or merchant were eager to join the army and fight to save their families and city or town.

Jehan and his brothers Symon and Denys Le Plastrier, although young, were among the brave men who fought hard with gunpowder and crossbows. But despite the determination of the citizens, aided by English and German reinforcements, it was a disaster when Rouen finally fell a month later. It was a bloody battle ending with thousands of bodies lying without dignity in a field of blood. Crushed and twisted limbs lay entangled, one body piled on top of the other. It was estimated that over three thousand men were captured and put to the sword by the royalists during the battle. Étienne Pasquier reflected gloomily, 'It would be impossible to tell you what barbarous cruelties are committed by both sides.'[16]

The fighting was frenzied, and the royalist leaders took senseless and irresponsible risks. Antoine was especially reckless and fought on the front line without his helmet. He was wounded by a musket while removing his trousers to relieve himself, and make lewd gestures to the men who were defending the city from the ramparts. He later died at nearby Les Andelys. Even as he was near death, he could not make up his mind whether to die Catholic or Protestant, but eventually decided that the latter was a better bet. He left behind his estranged wife, Jeanne d'Albret, their three-year-old daughter Catherine and their nine-year-old son, Henri.

After the city fell my ancestors were in even greater danger of losing their lives, homes, and businesses, as the king ordered his soldiers to persecute every Huguenot that they could lay their hands on. Goldsmiths were especially targeted, as guilds were considered a threat to the realm. Joined as usual by Catholic mobs, soldiers went about their business with glee. Homes were desecrated, and work tools vandalised. Fortunately, they were forewarned and many including my ancestors survived, as did the hastily prepared Table of Copper with the names of the current members, including Jehan Le Plastrier. Some converted or fled in fear and settled in safer towns or cities. The stalwart Le Plastriers chose to remain.

Undeterred by the continual setbacks, the exhausted Huguenots continued fighting for liberty with fortitude and fervour. In December, the ever-confident Guise met the weaker Huguenot army in Dreux, about fifty miles west of Paris, but he underestimated their determination and perseverance. Coligny led charge after charge with such valour that his army captured the commander, Montmorency. After the loss of their much-revered leader most of the Catholic troops threw down their pikes and swords and fled.

Unfortunately, the admiral's triumph was short-lived. Resting on his laurels he ordered his troops to take a break, but his cavalry ignored him and began looting the deserted royalist troops' baggage. Seeing that the Huguenot leaders were without their cavalry, Guise seized the opportunity and regrouped his men. He unexpectedly appeared from the crest of a hill supported by his loyal pikemen, who thrust their long pikes into the unsuspecting Huguenots while Guise stormed into the fray full of bravado. Before Coligny had time to order his forces back into battle, those who survived were surrounded by their enemies. Condé was captured and later imprisoned. The battle lasted five hours and the bloodshed and carnage were appalling. It was a veritable charnel house. As the conflict and hostilities continued, Catherine was forced to revoke the Edict of January.

A year later, Guise boldly drove his troops towards the Huguenot citadel of Orléans, where he established a siege by capturing the surrounding areas in readiness to attack the town. Fortunately, the assault never transpired. One evening when he was returning to camp having inspected his troops, he was mortally wounded by an *arquebus* shot aimed by a nineteen-year-old youth from Saintonge, named

Jean de Poltrot. He was immediately captured and tortured until he confessed that Coligny had paid him to kill Guise. It is doubtful that the honourable, much-respected admiral would have stooped so low, but as the duke was shot in the back the Guises vowed to avenge his murder. Jeanne d'Albret, shocked that anyone could possibly think her friend Coligny responsible, wrote, 'he is falsely accused ... I cannot believe anything so vicious of a man so upright and straightforward as the said Admiral is recognised by everyone to be.'[17]

Coligny did admit to paying Poltrot to spy on the royalists but vehemently denied bribing him to kill Guise. Unfortunately, he could not resist adding, 'This death is the greatest good that could have happened to this kingdom and to the Church of God, and in particular to myself and my entire House.'[18] The remark did nothing to improve his relationship with the Guise family and their coreligionists. However, it is much more likely that Catherine was behind the killing. According to the *mémoires* of Gaspard de Tavannes, a Catholic military leader, after tearfully sprinkling holy water over her *bête noire's* coffin, 'she admitted that those de Guises planned to seize the throne, which she had well and truly prevented them from doing at Orléans.'[19] The Venetian ambassador concurred that the queen mother had said that 'if Monsieur de Guise had perished sooner, peace would have been made more quickly.'[20] Jean de Poltrot was later executed at the Place de Grève in Paris. He was tortured with red-hot pokers, before being drawn apart by four large warhorses and finished off by swords – another customary punishment visited on Huguenots.

The death of the formidable and influential duke changed everything for the better for Catherine, and to some extent for the Huguenots, but not for the extremist Catholics and the Parisians, who were thrown into disarray at the demise of their esteemed leader. They wanted Coligny's head without delay. They demanded justice, which was not forthcoming as Catherine refused to chastise him. She still felt more secure with her Huguenot allies, but with Antoine dead, Condé captured, and Jeanne d'Albret sheltering in Béarn, she knew that she had no option but to totally conform to Catholicism. If she played her cards well, she could regain her supremacy.

Huguenot leaders were ordered to leave court, and tutors and ministers were dismissed. Only Mass was heard and Catherine's children, who, apart from Marguerite, had been brought up as Protestant, were told to convert. With Guise in his grave and the dreaded Triumvirate now non-existent, in a bid to stop the warring and to reconcile the people Catherine signed the Edict of Pacification, on behalf of the king, in March 1563.

The edict was meant to cede a little more to the Huguenots but was less generous than the Edict of January, which had permitted them to preach anywhere outside town centres during daylight hours. Now they were restricted to a limited number of suburbs but, with permission, could hold services on the estates of Protestant nobles, although not on Sundays. Calvin accused Condé and Montmorency, who had agreed to the edict, of limiting Protestantism to the aristocracy. Members of *Parlement* were particularly opposed to what they saw as more concessions for the heretics, and, as always, refused to approve it, but eventually agreed to register it when Charles reached his majority.

In an effort to encourage Charles to become more autonomous, and to get the edict endorsed, Catherine decided not to wait until he was fourteen, which was the legal age of majority for a French king to inherit the right to rule and exercise the highest authority. *Parlement* refused to allow the thirteen-year-old king to hold the ceremony in Paris, thus Rouen was selected for this prestigious occasion which took place on a rainy day in August. The Le Plastriers, being loyal subjects, would have been among the crowds who flocked to line the cobbled streets to watch the spectacular pageantry. Charles IX arrived, resplendent, riding a gleaming black warhorse, his colourful doublet trimmed with precious stones, and wearing a black plumbed cap. He and his entourage were preceded by a fanfare of drums and trumpets followed by flag-bearers and knights holding banners, lavishly embroidered with the crests of the noble Houses of France, high above their heads. As promised, *parlement* grudgingly kept their word and registered the edict, which brought the first phase of the Wars of Religion to an end.

Much to his mother's disappointment Charles still showed little interest in governing the country; therefore Catherine, whose regency had officially ended, continued to preside over his council and make key decisions for most of his reign. Charles was academically clever and artful, but ineffectual, frail, and latterly showed signs of the mental instability that ran through the family. He was inclined to fly into sudden irrational rages, terrifying his courtiers and family. He was not particularly interested in sports or court entertainment, but when not on his sickbed loved to spend time hunting.

At the end of July, Montmorency and his army had successfully recaptured Le Havre from the English. Elizabeth was outraged, but peace terms were eventually agreed under the Treaty of Troyes signed in 1564 – not to be confused with the Treaty of Troyes of 1420 signed by Charles VI. This officially recognised French ownership in exchange for 120,000 gold crowns.

Four years of relative calm followed the Edict of Pacification, but regardless of the agreement neither side completely disarmed and Protestants continued to be persecuted. In retaliation they burned down churches, and eventually resorted to killing monks. With the Guise family and their adherents out of favour, following Machiavelli's teaching, Catherine attempted to steer a middle course. She hoped to keep the peace by welcoming her old friends including Coligny and Condé – recently released from prison – back to court. This did not deceive the Huguenots, who, ever wary of the queen mother, declared that 'the craftiness and malice of the said lady was so great that she delighted in causing division and hatred among the princes, setting them against one another in order that she might reign and thereby remain sole governess of her son and of the Kingdom.'[21]

Always aware of her majesty and importance, the queen mother lived extravagantly. This was partly to hide the dire state of the treasury, which continued intermittently throughout her sons' reigns. Undeterred by the tenuous state of the royal finances, Catherine's continued desire to emulate her father-in-law's sumptuous, glamorous, and extravagant court consumed her. Her châteaux were furnished with expensive thick Turkish carpets, oak chests, gilded panelling, and priceless tapestries. She delighted in ceremony and being surrounded by grandeur. Catherine and the king kept separate households, and both employed thousands of staff from nobles to lowly servants. Her lavish private chambers, in whichever château they were residing, were always open to *L'Escadron Volant* and her attendants, both male and female. She often travelled on horseback accompanied by at least fifty of her alluring ladies, all mounted on handsome stallions and dressed in fur-trimmed riding capes. Contrary to her rather decorous character, there was constantly some form of elaborate and spectacular entertainment taking place.

Catherine was fascinated by dwarfs and enjoyed arranging marriages between them, in the hope that they would produce more dwarfs. They lived in separate grand households with their own footmen, maids, and tutors. They were always expensively dressed in the finest furs and brocades, adorned with jewels. She loved animals and as well as her beloved horses and dogs, owned lions, bears, and many other exotic species.

Unlike many royal and aristocratic ladies, she astutely preferred to dress in black, thus providing the best background to show off her priceless furs and sparkling gems, worn on special occasions. She was normally attired in a voluminous skirt with a long, pointed bodice, and enormous puffed, frilly sleeves; her neck adorned with a white lace ruffle and a high-standing collar. A long mantle fell from the back of the collar.

It was common knowledge that the queen mother dabbled in the occult, which did not help her popularity or credibility. She kept broken mirrors, crushed plumes, and broken chains, as a sign of relinquishing pomp, and regularly held secret psychic meetings led by her esteemed astrologer, an Italian named Cosimo Ruggieri. In a darkened room he regularly gazed into Catherine's magic looking glass searching for the latest prophecy, mainly regarding the life expectancy of her sons. He also mixed strange and, it was whispered, occasionally poisonous potions.

CHAPTER EIGHT

The Grand Royal Tour

Actually, being feared is perfectly compatible with not being hated.[1]

Niccolò Machiavelli, *The Prince*

Catherine sensed that radical measures were now desperately needed to save the realm. In an effort to establish the ties of loyalty to Charles and to uphold the Edict of Pacification, she and the fifteen-year-old king set out on a long, extravagant tour of the provinces with an entourage of several thousand. They left Paris on 24 January 1564, accompanied by the entire royal household, members of the court with their servants, and a military escort. The extensive caravan formed a veritable city on the march as carriages travelled along rough roads, through freezing cold, rain, and blazing heat. They stopped at provincial towns, cities, and picturesque villages along the way, staying in châteaux, palaces, and abbeys.

The grandiose entourage included low and high-ranking nobles, priests, government officials, astrologers, poets, physicians, trumpeters, lyre players, cooks, ladies-in-waiting, *L'Escadron Volant*, and the king's Groom of the Stool – one of the most sought-after positions at court, usually given to a noble of the inner sanctum. The vocation of this favoured aristocrat was to clean the monarch's posterior with stool *ducketts* – reusable cloths. He was accompanied by a trusted assistant bearing a bejewelled, velvet-seated commode for the king's evacuations.

Attendants led the way, carrying gold-studded chests containing valuable jewels, fine clothing, and bed linen, along with cloth of gold, tapestries, furniture, gold plate, and everything needed for their constant feasts and entertainment. Hundreds of horses required for jousting and hunting, together with their grooms, followed the convoy. There were tournaments, hawking, masked balls, concerts, royal tennis, carnivals, and lavish banquets. No expense was spared.

The bystanders and townspeople must have been awestruck as this magnificent procession passed them by displaying splendid, opulent carriages occupied by royalty and nobles. They were accompanied by Catherine's adored dwarfs in their own plush miniature carriages; the whole procession led by a fanfare of trumpets, drums, and flutes.

The queen mother hoped to vindicate her previous Protestant alliances, and to discuss marriage proposals for her younger children with a face-to-face meeting in Bayonne with her daughter Elisabeth and her powerful son-in-law. However, the meeting with Philip never materialised as he had no wish to meet *Madame la Serpente*, as he allegedly called her behind her back, or the insipid young king. Catherine's earlier dependence on the Huguenot hierarchy as political allies had made the Spanish king highly suspicious and distrustful of her. Instead, he sent his chief advisor, the ruthless, black-garbed General Fernando Álvarez de Toledo, Duke of Alba, as his personal representative.

Philip refused to allow Elisabeth to meet her mother unless she guaranteed that his wife would not come into contact with a heretic. There were many prominent Protestants accompanying the king. All were instructed to vacate the area while Catherine entertained the Spanish dignitaries. They were furious, especially as Alba, the most hated and feared of all men by the Huguenots, was the honoured guest. It was suspected that some monstrous plot was in the air. Espionage was prevalent, and they had a network of spies who would report back to them.

Elisabeth, accompanied by Alba and a large escort of Spanish nobles, eventually arrived in Bayonne mounted on a splendid, gleaming black palfrey, its harness encrusted with precious gems. After the ritual of exchanging expensive gifts, the festivities and entertainments began with a spectacle of extravaganzas. The guests were ferried on ornately decorated gilded barges, accompanied by musicians, down the Bidasoa River to an island where the celebrations took place. Stunning tableaux were performed on either side of the river along the route to keep the guests amused.

Once on the island, which had been designed to resemble a meadow, the royal family sat at a table placed on an elevated platform under an ornate canopy. Guests were seated in a circle below at elegantly laid tables of twelve arranged in individual niches. They were served on gold plates by 'shepherdesses dressed in cloth of gold and satin, after the fashion of the different provinces of France... The entire company was serenaded by a large troop of musicians, habited like satyrs, seen to come out of the opening of a rock, well lighted up, whilst nymphs were descending from the top in rich habits, who, as they came down, formed into a grand dance...'[2]

The *pièces de résistance* on each table at the banquet were enormous peacocks their stunning feathers and beaks edged in gilt. On either side were tall silver cages filled with small, colourful, chirping birds, their feathers and feet also dipped in gilt. At the end of each table were large, silver-edged savoury pies with smaller pies piled up around them to form a crown, also heavily gilded and lavishly decorated at the top.

The copious feast consisted of several courses, each beautifully displayed: civet of hare presented in ornate gold jugs, a whole salted stag, stuffed chickens, *fricassée* of veal served with sugarplums, roe deer, goslings, capons, pigeons, and wild boar, all served with rich sauces.

The meal ended with jellies and sweet pastries shaped into swans and stags, their necks having the royal coat of arms iced onto them; sweet creams and plums stewed in rose water... and so it continued. Wine flowed from the many fountains which had been erected for the purpose. Just as the spectacular ball was about to commence at the end of the *coupe de théâtre*, the heavens opened – a catastrophe!

Catherine had hoped to convince Philip that peace treaties were essential to end the religious problem, partly by forming marital alliances between the Valois and the Habsburgs. She was optimistic that Philip would agree to a marriage between Anjou and his widowed sister Juana, dowager queen of Portugal, and to Marguerite marrying Philip's son and heir, Don Carlos. It had seemingly slipped her mind that Juana was old enough to be Anjou's mother, and that Don Carlos was mentally unstable.

The queen mother was astounded when Alba announced that Philip was indifferent to world peace, and royal marriages. He declared that the king considered the rise of Protestantism in France to be a serious threat to his kingdom and desired it to be extinguished before it had a chance to pervade his realm. Protestantism was the recognised religion in England and many parts of Germany and Switzerland, and was now spreading in the predominantly Catholic Netherlands, part of Philip's dominion. Alba warned Catherine that if she refused to eliminate the Huguenot leaders, with the aim of completely obliterating heterodoxy in France, Philip would deal with them for her.

After the shedding of many public tears and the wringing of hands, the queen mother finally agreed. But she did not intend to keep to her promise quite yet, as the Huguenots were in a strong position and she still hoped that peace could be achieved by other methods. But this toadying of hers would have far-reaching ramifications.

CHAPTER NINE

Escalation Of Oppression

The contender who is not your ally will always try to get you to fight.[1]

Niccolò Machiavelli, *The Prince*

The weary party of the Grand Tour finally returned to Paris after almost two years of travelling. The information reported back to the Huguenots, who had been excluded from the festivities and talks at Bayonne, was bewilderingly inconclusive and rumours and innuendo abounded that the meeting had been arranged to discuss a plan to totally exterminate them. It would be impossible to overstate their fear and mistrust of Catherine and the Spanish king.

The Huguenots' concerns were reinforced later that year by an outbreak of appalling brutality in the Netherlands against Protestants – later known as the *Counseil Des Troubles* after an iconoclastic outbreak by the growing number of Protestants. The violence soon spread to Flanders where thousands were massacred by the Spanish army, led by the tyrannical Alba. 'The Huguenots say that she [Catherine] has given them fine words and feigned welcomes, while all the time she has been treating with the Catholic King and scheming their destruction. The Catholics, on the other hand, declare that if she had not exalted and favoured the Huguenots, these latter would not have been able to do what they have.'[2] Deeply divided, France was hovering on the edge of destruction.

In fact, Catherine did not trust the Spanish king one bit and was almost as terrified of Alba as the Huguenots were. The herculean Spanish army, led by the latter, was passing along the border of France on the way to the Netherlands, where Philip intended to increase repression. As a precaution, Catherine supplemented the royal army with some five thousand pike-wielding Swiss mercenaries, who were regarded as the finest warriors in Europe.

The realm's finances were in a critical state after the enormous cost of the Grand Tour. Catherine had already borrowed thousands of *écus* from the Gondi Bank, but more financial help was needed to cover the cost of the extra troops. The Cardinal de Lorraine was the only person in the kingdom with enough influence with the pope to raise sufficient funds, leaving the queen mother with no choice but to invite him back to court. Apart from needing financial aid, it would show Philip and the Parisians how strong her commitment to the Catholics was. Aided and abetted by the Duc d'Anjou she began implementing her plan by dismissing her loyal mentor and chancellor Michel de l'Hôpital, whose advice she had relied on for so many years, and replacing him with her old enemy.

The exultant cardinal arrived at Amboise, bringing with him his radical supporters and an exceptionally charming and handsome young blond Adonis – his nephew Henri, son of François, Duc de Guise, who was assassinated at Orléans in 1563. Wearing her mask of friendship, the conniving Catherine ingratiated herself with her august guests. Since childhood Anjou had loathed the young duke, as he had never forgotten how he had tried to persuade him to leave his family and live with his sister Claude, but he was delighted to see the cardinal again as he hated the Huguenots as much as Anjou.

The recall of her adversary is another indication of the queen mother's Machiavellian strategy of discarding those who are no longer of use to her. But the return of the extremist cardinal to his former position on the royal council was the last straw for the Huguenot leadership.

The cardinal wasted no time in cementing his power and argued for more draconian laws and increased oppression of the Huguenots. In despair, Condé issued a statement explaining that 'the reason why the King's subjects cannot live in peace and liberty of conscience as he wants them to do, is the friendship between the Duke of Anjou and the Cardinal of Lorraine and you can assure the King that I will not enter his court as long as the Cardinal of Lorraine remains there.'[3] Referring to the Guises, Coligny wrote that they were the 'source, root, and origin of the ruin and subversion which menaces this crown.'[4]

Jeanne d'Albret, desperate to rescue her beloved fourteen-year-old son, Henri, finally managed to extricate him from the clutches of the cardinal and the queen mother, who was furious. She took him to the safety of La Rochelle, where many Huguenots were gathered in fear of their lives. Despite living with the royal family for most of his life, Henri had maintained his Protestant beliefs and was only too happy to join the mother he adored. With the departure of Jeanne and her son, Catherine's former friends were now completely estranged from her and from court life.

Crucially, the peace edict was supposed to be in place to safeguard the Huguenots. Coligny again wrote disdainfully to Catherine, 'It must be confessed that if you have the good will you have not the power.'[5] The mass-murdering Alba's reign of terror, the arrival of the Swiss mercenaries, together with the cardinal's return, convinced the Huguenots that their suspicions were correct and that there was a scheme to eliminate them. The admiral, always loyal to the king, was concerned that Charles could once again come under the villainous influence of the Guises.

Thus, in September 1567, in an intrigue that echoed that of the Conspiracy of Amboise seven years earlier, the Huguenot army led by Condé tried, unsuccessfully, to kidnap Charles. Unaware of the plot, the royal family were residing at the château de Montceaux in Brie near Meaux, where they planned to hunt wild boar. Their spies eventually got wind of the ambush, known as the *Surprise de Meaux*, and it was foiled at the last minute but not before the family were thrown into total panic. Catherine and the distraught king narrowly escaped to Paris under cover of darkness, followed by their alarmed, disarrayed, and dishevelled courtiers, some on horseback and others on foot.

Undeterred, the Huguenot army remained in Saint-Denys, which had recently been captured by them, and prepared to besiege Paris. Eventually, the seventy-four-year-old Anne de Montmorency and his soldiers emerged through the city gates to meet the waiting troops, and battle commenced. Condé and his army, who were short of heavy armour and artillery, almost won the day having determinedly led charge after charge, but the royalists held sway and they were forced to retreat. Having led his men to victory, Montmorency was wounded in the battle and died two days later. Catherine was delighted – another enemy eliminated.

Condé wrote to the queen mother explaining that they had only wished to free the king from the cardinal's control, but she did not believe him. As the intended hostage was her son, the episode marked the culmination of her alleged moderate approach towards the Huguenots. She was convinced that they had betrayed the king and was determined to see them defeated, and their leadership annihilated as Alba had requested. From that day Catherine dispensed with any pretence and became their bitter enemy.

In another calculating move to prevent the Huguenots from besieging Paris, Charles, on instructions from his still-influential mother, signed a further peace agreement in the hope of tricking them into disbanding. Although suspicious that it had been signed by the 'puppet king', Huguenots preferred peace to war and immediately agreed to demobilise. Furious at Catherine's evident attempt to appease the heretics, fanatical Catholics continued to massacre them particularly in Paris, Rouen, Auxerre, Bourges, and Orléans.

In retaliation Huguenots pillaged and burned Catholic churches and strangled priests. Coligny branded it, that 'bloody peace full of infidelity.'[6]

Ignoring the bloodshed, Catherine wasted no time in putting a covenant on the lives of the Huguenot leaders. 'Her scheme was to seize Condé and Coligny. She hoped to be able to do this, as La Rochelle, which had refused to accept a Catholic governor, gave her a specious pretext under which to mature her plans.'[7] With coded messages and espionage from one side to the other, they soon discovered her imminent intention to have them murdered and planned accordingly. To warn their allies when the evil plan was due to be executed, they created a code, 'The stag is in the net, the hunt is ready.'[8] On receiving the warning, Condé and Coligny gathered up their families and servants before fleeing to the safety of La Rochelle. François de La Rochefoucauld, François d'Andelot, and other chief Huguenots also received the message and fled their homes.

The heavily fortified city of La Rochelle was virtually operated as a mini state by the Huguenots. The port was almost impregnable as it was protected on three sides by water, which was useful as it acted as a strategic harbour for diplomatic access to England and the Netherlands. The city could only be accessed by land from the north, which was not easy either as it was protected by massive high walls and towers.

From the safety of their citadel, they encouraged their supporters throughout the country to rally the fighting men, who had dispersed after the feigned peace agreement. The rank and file did not fail them. At the first summons to arms, 'with a joy and ardour incredible, they abandoned their wives, their children, their homes, and came in daily to join the Prince,'[9] many having travelled vast distances. The royalists also prepared for war but were unable to muster an army as fast, because they were insolvent.

Huguenots were now stronger and better funded, as they had military leaders such as the admiral, who was the most respected cavalry commander in the kingdom. He and the influential Condé used their many contacts with sympathetic Protestant countries, namely England and Germany, for aid. The German princes loaned them their fierce troops, known as *Reiters*, and Elizabeth financed them in return for jewels pledged by Jeanne d'Albret, and other Huguenot ladies.

The death of Montmorency left the royalists without a commander, and the king hoped that the honour might be given to him and not his younger brother Anjou. He pleaded with his mother, 'Young as I am, Madame, I feel that I am strong enough to bear my own sword, and if it were not so, would my brother, who is younger than I, be any more suitable?'[10] His words fell on deaf ears. In a moment of madness, Catherine had promoted the inexperienced sixteen-year-old Anjou to lieutenant general. He was now in command of the kingdom's entire armed forces. This caused further animosity among the already estranged and warring royal brothers.

Anjou had been brought up Protestant when Catherine had been under the Huguenots' spell, but was now a committed Catholic and eager to fight against them. Initially, he was not a good leader, and when it became obvious that the hugely depleted royalists were under pressure from Condé's army, the tough military strategist Gaspard de Tavannes was commissioned to his aid – they eventually proved a formidable team.

To protect their bastion, the Huguenot strategy was to fortify the south-west and hold the royalists at bay. They laid siege to several cities in the Poitou and Saintonge regions and captured Angoulême and Cognac. In March 1569, notwithstanding their superior army, they met their match at Jarnac near Cognac. The valiant and faithful Condé charged into the melee bellowing, 'For Christ and country!'[11] He was so intent on winning the battle that he found himself separated from his men, injured, his horse dead beneath him, and surrounded by enemies. He immediately surrendered but was fatally shot in the back by a Catholic assailant, rumoured to be on the orders of Anjou.

The latter, the nominal leader of the royalists in this battle, showed his true character and delighted in the unscrupulous murder of the prince. He callously slung Condé's butchered body onto an emaciated old donkey, before contemptuously parading it through the streets of Jarnac to shouts and jeers of joy. 'In both camps bloodthirstiness was only matched by their desire to insult one another. Death was no more respected than life. They lived only for hatred, without being able to satisfy it, according to the atrocious laws of civil war.'[12]

Théodore-Agrippa d'Aubigné, the Huguenot chronicler, who witnessed the battle, remembered, 'It was the fiercest and most stubborn combat of the civil wars. Among others we noticed an old man named La Vergne, who fought that day in the midst of twenty-five nephews, he and fifteen of them being slain, all in a heap.'[13] .

The cold-blooded queen mother, having conveniently forgotten that Condé had once been her mentor and friend, showed no grief at his demise, just great pleasure. She and her retinue eagerly left Paris and travelled for over three days to congratulate her beloved son on his glorious achievement at Jarnac. Although Condé was a prince of the blood and a cousin of the king, the royal family, the Guises, and ultra-Catholic Parisians were elated at his murder and there were many celebrations at court.

Condé's first wife was Eléonore de Roye, who died in 1654, but at the time of his death he was married to Françoise d'Orleans-Longueville. They had three sons and were living in their main residence, Château de Vallery. The murder of their revered and fearless royal figurehead was a severe setback for the Huguenots. The admiral now stood alone as military commander, but he and his coreligionists were determined to continue fighting for their freedom as Condé would have desired.

Coligny took the two young fatherless princes Henri de Bourbon – Antoine and Jeanne's son – and Condé's fifteen-year-old son by his first wife Eléonore, also named Henri, under his wing and trained them as future leaders and negotiators. They eventually formed an alliance with the Protestant Louis of Nassau in the Netherlands, who was fighting for the independence of the United Provinces from Spain with his younger brother William of Orange. The Guises meanwhile became increasingly allied with Philip.

Soon after the battle at Jarnac the Spanish ambassador Francés de Álava, who had replaced Catherine's adversary Chantonnay, aware that the queen mother reputedly had a habit of ridding herself of her enemies by poison, steel, or assassins, suggested that the time had come to carry out her promise to Alba and eradicate the Huguenot leaders. Catherine replied that she had already put a price on the heads of several prominent heretics. Not long after this admission, the admiral's youngest brother François d'Andelot died at Saintes, and Coligny and François de La Rochefoucauld simultaneously became extremely ill.

It was rumoured that d'Andelot had been poisoned. Coligny's other brother Ôdet, who had escaped to England, was also allegedly murdered by poisoning. His body rests in the Trinity Chapel in the east end of Canterbury Cathedral. There were several other unsuccessful attempts to kill Coligny, but he had a network of spies who kept him forewarned and was constantly vigilant. Frustrated that her repeated attempts to eradicate the admiral failed, Catherine persuaded Charles to condemn him to death in absentia, and to strip him of all his titles, honours, and estates.

In early October 1569, Anjou, Tavannes, and their troops, supplemented by Swiss mercenaries, engaged the Huguenot army in a battle near Montcontour, north-west of Poitiers, but the Huguenots were no match for the Swiss pikemen and the admiral was badly wounded. Undeterred by the heavy casualties and his injury, Coligny and his men continued to hold their own in further battles. Although most of his infantry was lost, his cavalry remained almost intact. To exact revenge, the insecure and unpredictable king ordered the royalists to lay a cowardly siege on Saint-Jean-d'Angély, where many unarmed and exhausted Huguenot soldiers were resting. Almost all were killed that day. Coligny again attempted to remind Catherine that a peace agreement was supposed to be in place and wrote, 'God will not leave unpunished the shedding of so much innocent blood, which cries continually before Him for vengeance.'[14]

When Coligny, who had not been among those taking refuge in Saint-Jean-d'Angély, heard about the irrational slaughter he was determined to strike back. He regrouped his men, supplemented by a corps of German cavalry, and attacked principal Catholic towns including Toulouse, Montpellier, and Carcassonne. The royalists had lost so many men that they were unable to retaliate.

The number of Huguenots had massively increased over the years, particularly in western and southern France, although the Parisians and the majority of the poorer people remained loyal and resolute Catholics. Regardless of their casualties in the previous battles, the Huguenots were in a strong defensive position as they now controlled, among others, the fortified towns of Montauban, Cognac, La Rochelle, and La Charité-sur-Loire. As they progressed towards Paris, Coligny and his company were again successful when they met the royalists in the small town of Arnay-le-Duc, south-west of Dijon.

The morale of the royal army was low, and to prevent the Huguenots from acquiring more towns and cities, Charles reluctantly signed the Peace of Saint-Germain-en-Laye in August 1570. Jeanne d'Albret, who had been lobbying persistently for justice for years, played a large part in the peace talks although she was sceptical of any input from Catherine or the king:

> It stated that such nobles as were in possession of 'high justice', and they only, were to enjoy the right of worship in their houses. As for the rank and file – Protestant services could be held in all towns which had been in the hands of the Huguenots from the 1st of August, and in the suburbs of two others in each government. In addition, Huguenots could refuse the jurisdiction of the hostile Parlement of Toulouse. But the one really important concession was that four towns – La Rochelle, Cognac, Montauban, and La Charité – were to be held for two years as security for the strict observance of the edict. Thus, for the first time French Protestantism had a separate political existence.[15]

Now that money for arms and troops were no longer required, neither was the cardinal and the Guises had once again fallen from grace. Needless to say, the armistice aroused nothing but distrust and grievances from both sides. The Catholics thought the Edict had conceded far too much, and the Huguenots that it had not gone far enough. They suspected that it was signed to deceive them and silence their fears, while Anjou and his mother continued with their plan to finally eradicate them.

CHAPTER TEN

The Marriage Conspiracy

*Hence, if a ruler wants to survive, he'll have to learn to stop
being good, at least when the occasion demands.*[1]

Niccolò Machiavelli, *The Prince*

C harles showed none of the leadership, glory, or majesty of
his predecessors and his irrational rages became ever more
frequent. He still relied heavily on his mother and was
extremely envious of her obsessive love for Anjou. In the past he
would have agreed to anything to win her approval, but now that he
was twenty-one that influence was diminished.

The queen mother became increasingly unpopular as she constantly
prevaricated, and the people lost all respect for her. She was still
planning to destroy the Huguenot leadership, but was conscious of
the kingdom's financial difficulties and the continuing importance of
being perceived to be neutral.

As the realm was relatively peaceful and her nefarious plan was
on hold, Catherine returned to planning advantageous marriages
for her younger children. Having failed to procure a marriage

between Anjou and Juana, sister of Philip, her next choice was Queen Elizabeth, but Anjou dismissed the idea because she was too old, and a Protestant. Disappointed, she proposed her youngest son, the pockmarked, hunchbacked François d'Alençon – later Duc d'Anjou – who was leaning towards Protestantism. Despite the age difference and his unattractive appearance, Elizabeth seemed to become very fond of Alençon and for a time seriously considered him as a possible husband. She nicknamed him her 'frog', on account of a frog-shaped gold earring that he had sent her as a gift from Boulogne. Due to pressure from her privy council and the English public at large, who were not supportive of the union owing to anti-Catholic and anti-French sentiments, Elizabeth eventually turned him down in 1581.

Catherine's first choice of husband for her daughter Marguerite had been Philip's eldest son Don Carlos, but he had mysteriously died two years previously. She then set her sights on Sebastian, the sixteen-year-old religious ascetic king of Portugal, but he was more interested in reading Thomas Aquinas and carried a copy everywhere attached to his belt. His inseparable companions were two monks of the Theatines Order who were determined to protect him and viewed the House of Valois as far too tolerant of Protestants. After much conniving, Catherine decided that Henri de Bourbon, despite him being a heretic, would make a suitable husband for Marguerite. He had lived at court for much of his life and was a prince of the blood. Many Catholics would not be happy, but the queen mother had an ulterior motive.

Catherine wasted no time. She invited Jeanne d'Albret, her son, Henri, and daughter, Catherine, to visit her at Blois as soon as possible, explaining, 'the King, my son, [intends] to embrace the affairs of the Prince of Navarre [Henri], whom the King and I infinitely desire to see here, with you.'[2] Jeanne, having experienced the queen mother's deception in the past, suspected that some execrable plot was in the making and kept vacillating, but as the invitation was from the king, it was an order.

The admiral on the other hand was desperate to be reconciled at court so that he could have access to Charles, which would enable him to further his plan of waging war with Spain. Although still not welcome, he was less restricted after the peace agreement. With the king's blessing, Coligny and his son-in-law Charles de Téligny, together with some of their aristocratic Huguenot associates including François de la Nöue and François de La Rochefoucauld, had contrived the plan between them.

The idea was to encourage stability in France by taking up arms against Spain to free the Protestants in the Netherlands who were opposed to their barbarous overlord, Philip. If successful the Netherlands would become part of France, thus strengthening the weak economy and the power of the Huguenots. Charles was eager to become involved, as it was a chance for him to assert his authority. Since childhood his ambition had been to lead his army into victorious combat, and to show his mother and his subjects that he was a fearless, warrior king. This was his opportunity. He warned his partisans, 'there is one thing against which we must be on our guard. My Mother, the Queen likes to nose into everything, as you know, she must not be informed of this enterprise, or at least not of its full scope.'[3] For their dream to come to fruition, they needed more help from Germany and England. The German princes were always happy to loan their *Reiters*, but the parsimonious Queen Elizabeth was renowned for driving a hard bargain.

Unaware of Catherine's marriage plans, Coligny's idea was to propose a marital alliance between the English queen and Henri de Bourbon. This seemed the perfect solution as Henri was not unattractive, and a Protestant. He would one day be king of Navarre and was in line to the throne of France. Elizabeth was more likely to assist them if the two countries were allied by marriage. Coligny had the king's support, but he needed admittance to court, and that was impossible without the queen mother's seal of approval.

Catherine was totally opposed to the Netherlands offensive, of which she was aware, and was furious when she discovered that

Coligny and his associates were surreptitiously negotiating a possible marriage between Elizabeth and Henri. It had to be stopped. She pleaded with Charles, 'You hide yourself from me, who am your mother, in order to take counsel of your enemies; you wrench yourself from my arms, which have guarded you, to lean on the arms of those who once desired to kill you. I know that you hold secret counsels with the Admiral – that you wish to plunge us rashly into war with Spain...'[4]

The king was totally under Coligny's spell, and his mother was powerless. Charles was determined that his friend should return to court, therefore, Catherine had no option but to reluctantly agree. By playing her cards right she could prevent him from going to war with Spain, stop talks of a marital alliance with England, and end Coligny's friendship with the king. Hence, she reluctantly invited him to Blois.

The invitation was eagerly accepted, despite warnings from friends and family that the royal family was unscrupulous and murderous, and that he was likely to be imprisoned or beheaded. Disregarding their advice, he knew that the only way of succeeding with his plan was to gain access to the king. 'Better to die by a bold stroke than to live a hundred years in fear,'[5] he declared. Nevertheless, to be on the safe side he obtained a promise from Charles, who was delighted to have his old friend back, that he would not be in any danger from Catherine or her younger sons Anjou and Alençon.

The historic meeting took place at the queen mother's bedside at Blois in September 1571. Coligny, dressed in black with gold embellishments adorning his doublet, and a starched white ruff around his neck, was courteously welcomed by Catherine but without the normal kiss. It was the custom for queens of France to greet distinguished officers of the crown with a kiss on the mouth. He rode away five weeks later, unharmed, his precious forfeited estates of Châtillon returned, a cash bequest of one thousand *livres* in his pocket, and the privileged honour of fifty nobles to escort him wherever he desired, but more importantly an entrée to Charles's court. He was now in a position to influence him and to try to save his country and the Huguenots from disaster.

The king had known, admired, and respected Coligny since he was a boy when Huguenot nobles were welcomed at court, and still referred to him as *Mon Père*. The two men spent much time together discussing their plan. The admiral 'is to be found each day at the rising of the King, as well as when he dines and sups,' a courtier complained. 'At all hours he is close to his chair, and with the same freedom as those who never left court. And the King reasons and discourses with him as he does with the rest so that it seems as if the past were buried in perpetual oblivion.'[6]

Controversially, Coligny was again given huge power by being readmitted into the king's council. This appalled the extremist Catholics and Guise adherents. They continued to view Huguenots as heretics who refused to attend Mass, destroyed valuable relics, and attacked Catholic churches. They were also, erroneously, convinced that the Huguenot hierarchy were planning to seize overall power in France, and that all Catholics would be exterminated, or even worse forced to convert. The situation had become a crisis. In defiance of the new peace edict, armed rioters continued to massacre Huguenots.

The queen mother and Anjou become increasingly concerned about Charles's growing friendship with so many high-ranking Huguenots, especially with his mentor. Catherine regretted inviting him back to court and did her best to poison their friendship, but Coligny was growing increasingly influential and even more determined to declare war against Spain. In the queen mother's sinful mind, it was becoming clear that he must be eradicated without delay.

Part of her strategy was to ensure that the marriage between Marguerite and Henri de Bourbon went ahead as soon as possible. Coligny was quite happy to change his plan and assist Catherine to arrange a marriage between her youngest son Alençon and Queen Elizabeth, leaving the way open for Henri to marry Marguerite. Either way, a marital alliance between France and England would be achieved and help him to reach his ultimate goal.

Catherine wrote repeatedly to Jeanne requesting her to bring her children to Blois and, strangely, promised not to harm them. 'I cannot imagine why you should find it necessary to say that you want to see me and my children, but not in order to do us harm,' Jeanne replied caustically. 'Forgive me if I laugh when I read these letters, for you are allaying a fear I have never had. I have never thought that you fed on little children, as they say.'[7] She was passionately against the proposed marriage, as Marguerite was a devout Catholic and she and her son were ardent Huguenots.

She finally capitulated and arrived at the Château in March 1572 with ten-year-old Catherine, but without Henri. She was extremely suspicious of the queen mother's motives and was determined that she would not be forced into agreeing to the marriage. While at Blois Jeanne wrote a series of letters to her son. She conceded that her prospective daughter-in-law Marguerite, or Madame as she called her, was beautiful if remote. Rather acerbically she commented, 'as for the beauty of Madame, I admit she has a good figure, but it is too tightly corseted. Her face is spoiled by too much makeup, which displeases me...'[8]

Being deeply pious, Jeanne was shocked to witness Charles's licentious court and wrote, 'Not for anything on earth would I have you come to live here... Although I knew it was bad, I find it even worse than I feared. Here women make advances to the men rather than the other way around. If you were here, you would never escape without special intervention from God. The men cover themselves with jewels. The king recently spent one hundred thousand écus on gems and buys more every day.'[9]

Jeanne was caught in a web of cruelty and deceit. Initially, she was hopeful that the marriage had potential, and that she could persuade Marguerite to convert. But she soon accepted the fact that her future daughter-in-law had no intention of recanting her strong faith. While at Blois, Anjou and Catherine put inestimable pressure on Jeanne to coerce her to agree to the marriage. She complained that among other torments 'they scratch me, they stick pins into me, they flatter me, they tear out my fingernails, without letup... I am badly lodged; holes have been drilled in the walls of my apartment. I do not know how I can stand it. I have made up my mind to go no further.'[10] She fought hard but was forced to capitulate and was left with no option but to agree to the marriage when the king threatened to have Henri declared illegitimate by the pope. It was agreed that Henri could remain a Protestant – privately, Charles intended to force him to revoke his faith once the marriage had taken place.

Finally, Jeanne lamented to Henri, 'I am in agony, in such extreme suffering that if I had not been prepared it would overcome me... I am being obliged to negotiate quite contrary to my hopes and to their promises. I am not free to talk with either the King or Madame, only with the Queen Mother, who goads me... Monsieur [Anjou] tries to get around me in private with a mixture of mockery and deceit; you know how he is.'[11] Knowing that she had pledged her son to a brutal, depraved family, she rather endearingly advised him:

> I beg you to pay attention to three matters: be gracious, but speak boldly, even when you are taken aside by the King, for note that the impression you make on arrival will remain. The final thing is most on my mind. Every enticement will be offered to debauch you, in everything from your appearance to your religion... I know it is their object because they do not conceal it... try to train your hair to stand up and be sure there are no lice in it.[12]

Jeanne must have been relieved when the marriage contract was duly signed, and she could escape the excesses of Charles's depraved court, where nightly banquets and masked balls provided the opportunity for every possible promiscuous indulgence.

Three months later Jeanne was shopping in Paris for wedding gifts when she became ill and died. The autopsy revealed that the cause of death was tuberculosis, but as expected there was speculation that Catherine, who showed no sorrow at the demise of her former friend, had organised her murder. It was rumoured that she may have arranged for her death by sending a gift of poisoned gloves, provided by René Bianchi, the queen mother's Florentine *parfumier*. Jeanne's demise was a severe loss and setback to the Huguenots, and to Protestants in Europe. The Elector Palatine wrote, 'we are very distressed by it, but we accept God's will.' He added, ambiguously, 'she has trod the road we must all take… but if we had been present, we might have been able to prevent it.'[13] Had she lived, the terrible events following the wedding might also have been avoided.

Disregarding Jeanne's scathing comments, Marguerite's beauty, charm, and intelligence were legendary. After seeing her one Easter as she stepped out of her carriage, Brantôme wrote: 'her pure white face, resembling the skies in their serenity, was adorned about the head with quantities of pearls and jewels, equally brilliant diamonds, worn in the form of stars, so that the calm of the face and the sparkling jewels made one think of the heavens when starry. Her beautiful body with its full, tall form was robed in a gown of crinkled cloth of gold, the richest and most beautiful ever seen in France.' He added that 'she was more like a goddess of heaven than a princess of earth, for it is believed, on the word of several, that no goddess was ever seen more beautiful.'[14]

She was also adored by the dashing young Henri, Duc de Guise, who had lived for much of his childhood with the groom and the royal children. A marriage between Marguerite and the duke, both dedicated Catholics, would have caused much joy and celebration among the Parisians instead of anger and mistrust. It was common knowledge, but apparently not to the king or the queen mother, that Marguerite was involved in a long-standing clandestine liaison with Guise.

This changed after a spiteful courtier, the Marquis du Guast, a nephew of the cardinal, and one of Anjou's favourites, reportedly discovered Marguerite in a compromising position with her lover in a vacant chamber at the Louvre and reported the incident to the Spanish ambassador, who told Philip. When the queen mother and Charles, who was in one of his frequent demonic rages and did not need much encouragement, became aware of the situation they dragged Marguerite out of bed in the early hours. After pushing the poor girl into Catherine's chamber, mother and brother ripped her nightclothes into shreds, pulled her hair out in chunks, and beat her relentlessly. It was quite common in the sixteenth century for men of the family to act in a harsh manner towards their wives, daughters, and sisters, but not normally the mothers. The king warned the reluctant Marguerite that if she did not consent to the marriage, he would make her 'the most unhappy woman in the realm.'[15] The Guise family had allegedly supported and encouraged the romance, which infuriated Catherine.

Neither Marguerite nor Henri, now king of Navarre after the death of his mother, wished to marry as they had never particularly liked each other as children, and held such different and strong views on religion. Henri did not relish being married to a Catholic who was in love with another man, beautiful as she was. For her part, Marguerite was dismayed at the thought of leaving the splendour and excitement of her brother's court to spend the rest of her life in the austerity of Nérac – the capital of Navarre – surrounded by sombrely dressed Huguenots with high principles. She repeatedly begged her mother to reconsider, but it was a *fait accompli*. Much later, when her marriage was annulled, Marguerite's signed statement read:

> *Never did I consent willingly to this marriage… I was forced into it by King Charles IX and the Queen my mother. I besought them with copious tears, but the King threatened me that, if I did not consent, I should be the most unhappy woman in the realm. Although I had never been able to entertain any affection for the King of Navarre and said and repeated that it was my desire to wed another prince, I was compelled to obey. To my profound regret, conjugal affection did not exist between us during the seven months which preceded my husband's flight in 1575. Although we occupied the same couch, we never spoke to one another.[16]*

CHAPTER ELEVEN

St Bartholomew's Day Massacre

A ruler mustn't worry about being labelled cruel when it's a question of keeping his subjects loyal and united.[1]
Niccolò Machiavelli, *The Prince*

The marriage of Marguerite de Valois to Henri de Bourbon, King of Navarre, was part of Catherine's meticulously devised plan to use her daughter as a sacrificial lamb to lure the admiral and other prominent Huguenots to their fate. The conspiracy was so devious and complicated that it is difficult to correctly unravel. There is no doubt that her equally conniving son Anjou and the popular, charismatic Duc de Guise were all involved in the horrific massacre that followed. It is almost certain that the queen mother and Anjou ordered Coligny's murder, which initially failed, but whether Guise was a scapegoat in a political game or was involved in the plot from the onset is debatable.

It is hard to believe that Catherine or Anjou, who loathed the duke, would have deliberately involved him in the conspiracy. Yet, the Governor of Paris reported, 'In Paris there are a growing number of gentlemen friends of the lords of Guise, and they have rented rooms in various quarters, plotting nightly something between them… and that among the plans they have one will go and kill the Admiral.'[2]

The Guise family had always sworn to avenge Coligny for the murder of the former duke during the siege of Orléans in 1563. This occasion was perfect for retribution since the entire Huguenot leadership was staying in Paris for the wedding of Marguerite and Henri. Coligny was warned not to enter the city, which was Guise territory and simmering with religious tension, but he refused to be deterred. Nothing was going to stop him and his associates from supporting the momentous occasion of a marriage between a Huguenot and a beautiful Catholic princess. His beloved country would at last be at peace.

Catherine took an enormous risk in arranging the nuptials as the pope declined to grant dispensation, which was a prerequisite for royal Houses allied to the Vatican. She eventually managed to deceive the moderate Cardinal Charles de Bourbon into believing that she had received permission from the French ambassador in Rome.

Paris was in the midst of a heat wave and in the weeks leading up to the wedding the narrow, cobbled streets of the medieval city heaved with people from peasants to nobility. Catholics and Protestants of all classes travelled from every part of the country to witness the marriage. Most Huguenots were accommodated in inns and taverns, but those of high social rank stayed with their families as guests at the Louvre, or in nearby private residences. Almost all were destined to die a few days later.

The *hostelleries* were filled to capacity, and many people were forced to sleep by the stinking open gutters at the side of the streets amongst human waste, rats, drunks, and decomposing animals. As expected, the pope, the clergy, and the Parisians' hostility was palpable. They refused to accept the marriage of the popular princess to a heretic.

Seditious preaching full of acrimony, directed at Huguenots, was shouted from pulpits throughout the city interspersed with the joyous sound of the Huguenots chanting psalms.

A few days prior to the wedding the groom, attired in deep mourning on account of the death of his beloved mother, rode into Paris with an entourage of eight hundred Huguenots, all identically clothed. He was warmly welcomed and bestowed with every honour by Charles, who was delighted with the marriage and ordered that no expense should be spared. Parisians loved a spectacle, even if they were against the alliance.

Despite the reluctance of the bride and groom, the ceremony took place on the extremely hot morning of 18 August 1572. It was a prestigious occasion with Catholic and Protestant courtiers and honoured guests all extravagantly turned out. Regardless of the heat, ladies wore their finest brocade, or rich velvet gowns trimmed with ermine, and displayed their magnificent jewels saved for such special occasions. Some wore the entire value of their estates on their backs, but Huguenots preferred to dress more sombrely. Expensive black or white raised silk and muted velvet embellished with embroidery were popular.

The bride described her ensemble thus, 'I was set out in a most royal manner; I wore a crown on my head with the *coët*, or regal close gown of ermine, and I blazed in diamonds. My blue-coloured robe had a train to it of four ells [roughly fifteen feet] in length, which was supported by three princesses.'[3] Navarre, suitably resplendent in a pale yellow embroidered satin doublet and cape, thickly encrusted with pearls and diamonds, arrived with his retinue all similarly dressed. Although not very tall, he was much admired by Huguenot ladies for his good looks and charm.

It had previously been agreed that he would not have to enter the centuries-old Notre-Dame, or partake in the traditional nuptial Mass. Thus, the first part of the marriage ceremony was conducted on a specially constructed open-air platform, which was adorned with cloth of gold and led from the Bishop's Palace to the cathedral. Invited guests watched the proceedings from seated stands below, while the crowds jostled for space, perching on rooftops and window ledges.

Marguerite entered Notre-Dame to attend Mass alone, while the groom strolled up and down the platform talking animatedly to some of his Huguenot friends. Later, the new queen of Navarre and her husband appeared to the rapturous sounds emanating from many silver trumpets. Accompanied by the royal party, they entered the episcopal palace for a sumptuous banquet, followed by three days of grandiose festivities which continued until the early hours.

Most Huguenots were delighted with the marriage, and with the Peace of Saint-Germain-en-Laye. They felt that at last they were valued and accepted by the king for their loyalty. Nevertheless, they were aware that they had many enemies lurking in high places, as well as among the peasantry. Predictably, the truce was short-lived. Four days after the wedding, fighting and killings flared up again after an abortive attempt was made on Coligny's life. He was walking back from the Louvre to his Paris home in rue de Béthisy when a minor Catholic nobleman Charles de Louviers, Seigneur de Maurevert, known to Catherine and Anjou, fired a long-barrelled *arquebus* at him through the open window of an empty house said to be owned by the Guise family. This was obviously an attempt to kill the admiral but missed his vital organs and merely wounded him.

On hearing the news, an outraged Charles gathered up his leading physicians and rushed with his family to his friend's bedside where the royal surgeon, Ambroise Paré, removed a bullet from Coligny's elbow and amputated an injured finger. The king ordered the immediate arrest of Guise, who was the prime suspect, but he had disappeared. After the royal entourage had left, Coligny's family and supporters begged him to leave Paris. He refused, as Charles had given his word of honour that he would ensure his and his companions' safety during the celebrations. The king's word was good enough for him. Two leading Huguenots, Vidame de Chartres and the Compte de Montgomery, sensing trouble, decided to leave Paris and cross the river to their homes near Saint-Germain-en-Laye from where it would be easier to escape should this prove necessary. This decision saved their lives.

It was the misjudged murder attempt that triggered the horrendous massacre that was to follow – the worst in French history until the Revolution. Catholics now feared reprisals and began to covertly arm themselves. Catherine was concerned that should it become known that she and Anjou were involved in the failed attack on Coligny, they would be in great danger from the Huguenots. She had to think on her feet, and fast. There was no alternative but to confess her part in the attempted conspiracy to murder Coligny to the king, who had no knowledge of his mother and brother's involvement. But Catherine was too much of a coward to do this herself. Her daughter Marguerite remembered:

> *Accordingly, the Marshal [Duke of Retz] went to the King in his closet, between the hours of nine and ten, and told him he was come as a faithful servant to discharge his duty, and lay before him the danger in which he stood, if he persisted in his resolution of punishing M. de Guise, as he ought now to be informed that the attempt made upon the Admiral's life was not set on foot by him alone, but that his brother and the Queen his mother, had their shares in it.[4]*

Once the distraught, unstable, and vulnerable Charles had been made aware of the situation, Catherine, René de Birague, the Duc de Nevers, Gaspard de Tavannes, and Anjou, all entered his bedchamber to coerce and persuade him that the royal family now faced great danger. In a tissue of lies they accused the Huguenots of planning to seize power by killing him and overthrowing the House of Valois. Marguerite confirms, 'The Queen my mother used every argument to convince King Charles that what had been done was for the good of the State; and this because, as I observed before, the King had so great a regard for the Admiral, La Nöue, and Téligny [all Huguenots] on account of their bravery...'[5]

Charles did not believe them but eventually, under extreme

pressure, he screamed: 'Kill the lot! Kill the lot!'[6] Hence, in the early hours of 24 August, on the reluctant orders of the king, the bell, 'Marie', in the Church of Saint-Germain l'Auxerrois rang out signalling the death knell of all high-ranking Huguenots. This sequence of events later became known as the *Massacre de la Saint-Barthélemy*, as it was planned in Paris on the eve of the Feast of Bartholomew the Apostle.

It was normal for the royal family and courtiers to talk and party through the night, especially after a celebration. Much earlier that evening, Marguerite, unaware of the pressure being forced on the king, went to her mother's closet in the Louvre, but was thrown out. Her sister Claude, who was in floods of tears, begged her to remain, explaining that her life was in terrible danger if she left. But the callous queen mother ordered her daughter back to her own chambers, willingly sacrificing her to the mobs to save the lives of the rest of the family who were afraid of reprisals from Protestants. She was a danger to them because she was now married to one. Marguerite wrote, 'The Huguenots were suspicious of me because I was a Catholic, and the Catholics because I was married to the King of Navarre, who was a Huguenot.'[7]

On her way back she was summoned to join her husband and over thirty of his Huguenot friends. She spent the remainder of the night in his chamber, where he and his friends were discussing the attempted attack on Coligny and how to avenge Guise, who they assumed was responsible. Unaware of the horror awaiting them, they left at first light to join the king for a pre-arranged royal tennis match but were caught by his soldiers, who were waiting for them with swords and daggers in the courtyard of the Louvre. The dismayed Charles immediately regretted his orders and desperately attempted to halt the carnage. On seeing so many principal Huguenots, many of them his great friends, being horribly murdered in front of his eyes, he tried to save some but soon changed his mind, 'whereupon they were thrust out and massacred below almost to a man.'[8] Most of them great noblemen and fearless soldiers. The new Prince de Condé – son of Louis, who was murdered at Jarnac – and the groom, Navarre, survived, but not before they had watched in dismay and terror as their friends were slain.

The royal family remained barricaded in their private quarters, while listening in horror as the Louvre echoed with the screams of those trapped and terrified in the enemy fortress. Families were dragged from their beds, unsuspecting and half asleep. They had their throats cut before they had a chance to defend themselves. Women and girls, regardless of age, were raped before being butchered.

The Marquis de Renel, Baron de Pardaillan, Armand de Clermont, and the charming and popular François de La Rochefoucauld all lost their lives that morning. The latter was asleep when Chicot, the brother of the king's fool – court jester – and his masked assassins burst into his chamber. Thinking that the king had come to play a prank on him, as was often the case, he greeted them with joy and laughter. Instead, he was hacked to death. Charles de Téligny, Coligny's son-in-law, managed to escape onto the roof but was caught and killed with swords. François de La Nöue was one of the few Huguenot noblemen to survive.

Simultaneously, Admiral Gaspard de Coligny, the most adored and highly respected of Huguenot leaders, and such a great and loyal friend of the king, was hauled from his bed by officers of the royal guard and stabbed to death. As expected, this brave warrior, who had such a strong faith, met his fate with dignity and fearlessness. His body was derisively thrown out of the window into the filthy gutter, where it landed at the feet of the gloating Guise. The crowd mutilated and castrated him before pulling the body through the mud and throwing it into the Seine. Guise, doubtless innocent of the first attempt on Coligny's life, was only too happy to obey the king's command and complete the task. The admiral's remains now rest in his family residence, Château de Châtillon.

Having murdered every Huguenot they could find in the Louvre, the hate-filled soldiers began searching houses close by where many more guests were staying, mercilessly killing all they confronted. Fathers clinging to their children fought desperately, pistol in hand, to save them, yet it was hopeless. Baskets of dead babies and carts filled with the bodies of women, men, and children were carelessly thrown into the river, which was littered with corpses. Blood flowed through the rooms and courtyard of the Louvre, and down the cobbled streets of Paris.

Authentic accounts tell of infants who when grabbed by their assassins laughed and played with their captors' beards, before having their throats cut and being thrown into baskets. They tell of a young boy dragging a dead toddler, probably his sister, dressed in a beautiful long gown, through the streets at the end of a long piece of rope in order to throw the body into the river to save it from being ravaged. And of a beautiful woman, who had been stripped naked and raped by laughing mobs, standing terrified on a bridge before being recklessly thrown in the river to drown.

An Italian diplomat remembered passing by the Louvre early that morning, and seeing 'a dozen leading Huguenots dead or dying.' Two days later another [Italian diplomat] 'counted more than forty stretched stark naked on the ground.'[9] The killings threw everyone in Paris into total panic. They ran, many still in their nightclothes, to find shelter or a way of escaping but there was none as the gates of the walled city were locked and metal chains were used to block the streets.

Before the common people were even aware of the situation, the king ordered that all Huguenots should be murdered and robbed, not just the hierarchy. Soldiers and Paris mobs needed no encouragement. Identifiable by their plain, unadorned black-and-white clothes, they were stripped naked, tortured, disembowelled, and finally killed. 'Men and women died heroically rather than renounce their faith. Some tried to escape by wearing the Catholic badge of a white cross in the cap and a kerchief on the left arm, but as often or not they were recognised, or could not give the password.'[10] Father Panicarola gleefully wrote to Rome. 'Everywhere, we have seen rivers of blood and mountains of dead bodies.'[11] There were many Italian courtiers and diplomats in Paris who were thrilled by the death of so many

Protestants. But none of those involved in the collusion expected the carnage to be on such an enormous scale. Horrified, Guise declared his innocence, and that of his family, and rescued as many people as he could.

The lives of the admiral's family were saved as Coligny had insisted that his second wife Jaqueline de Montbel d'Entremont, four months pregnant, and the eight children from his first wife Charlotte de Laval, the love of his life, who died in 1568, remained in the safety of their home in Châtillon. Always on his guard, the admiral was aware that Guise blamed him for the murder of his father and was looking for retribution. The day after the massacre the king's knights arrived at the château and arrested the family. Some mercy was shown, perhaps by the king, as the youngest child Charles was later saved and grew up at court. All, apart from two of the servants, were imprisoned and Jaqueline and her stepdaughter Louise de Téligny were expelled from France. The older children had previously been sent to Switzerland under armed guard.

The bloodbath soon spread to other towns and cities including Rouen where the massacre lasted for months. Soldiers took full advantage of the signal from the king. They stormed through the towns in a frenzy of violence, horrifically killing every Huguenot they encountered. 'It was enough to cry, "There is a Huguenot!" to have a fresh victim.'[12] No mercy was shown to anyone; rich or poor. Men and women, in grand clothes or dressed in rags, children and infants – all were slayed. The stench was unbearable, with bodies left rotting in the gutters and streets, and the rivers stained with blood.

The violent armed rioters, having killed as many Protestants as possible, had a field day looting their houses and robbing clothes from bodies, leaving them naked and disfigured. Rouen endured more than most towns and cities, and the Huguenot community shrank by hundreds. Some Le Plastriers suffered but my ancestor Symon, who was thirty at the time, unmarried, and fortunately without children, miraculously survived. Many Huguenots converted or once again moved to safer towns and cities, but the Le Plastriers remained even more committed to fight for the freedom to practise their faith in peace.

The Huguenot movement was left badly crippled and vulnerable by the loss of so many influential members, but they were determined to continue defending their right for equality. Many of those who survived the bloodshed ceased to offer their allegiance to the king and became increasingly radicalised, while most Catholics were left shocked and horrified. There is no exact record of how many perished in the massacre, but it is thought to be at least three thousand in Paris alone during the first five days, and as many seven thousand throughout the rest of France. The reaction throughout Protestant Europe was one of disbelief and horror, which created greater solidarity.

At first Pope Gregory XIII and fanatical Catholics in France and abroad rejoiced – it was said that Philip of Spain laughed for the only time on record. When the pope heard the news, a special medal was struck to commemorate the glorious annihilation of the Huguenots and *Te Deums* were sung throughout Rome. The French ambassador speedily published a brief statement under a pseudonym, giving all the credit to the king entitled *The Stratagem of Charles IX*. However, when Pope Gregory and Philip learned that the queen mother and Anjou had planned the killing of Coligny and other leading Huguenots for political rather than religious reasons, they changed their tune. They now blamed the royal family for the deaths of so many innocent people for all the wrong reasons.

Marguerite had now served her purpose and Catherine pressured her into agreeing to annul her marriage. She didn't particularly like her new husband, and it is doubtful that the marriage had been consummated as Navarre had many mistresses and Charles's court was full of sexual opportunities. Nevertheless, Marguerite refused as she suspected that part of her mother and Anjou's overall scheme was to murder Navarre and the Prince de Condé. If she agreed to remain married, she hoped this could be avoided. She recalled:

Five or six days afterwards, those who were engaged in this plot, considering that it was incomplete whilst the King [of Navarre] my husband and the Prince of Condé remained alive, as their design was not only to dispose of the Huguenots, but of the Princes of the blood likewise; and knowing that no attempt could be made on my husband whilst I continued to be his wife, devised a scheme which they suggested to the Queen my mother for divorcing me from him. Accordingly, one holiday, when I waited upon her to chapel, she charged me to declare to her, upon my oath, whether I believed my husband to be like other men. 'Because said she, 'If he is not, I can easily procure you a divorce from him…' But said I, 'Madame, since you have put the question to me, I can only declare I am content to remain as I am;' and this I said because I suspected the design of separating me from my husband was in order to make some mischief against him.[13]

The two Huguenots narrowly avoided being assassinated thanks to Marguerite's intervention, and by pledging to convert. One month after the massacre, Navarre and Condé were forced to kneel before the altar at Notre-Dame to affirm their conversion to Catholicism in front of the king, Catherine, courtiers, and ambassadors. As the ceremony ended, the queen mother lost her customary dignity and burst into laughter. She was right to be sceptical as both intended to revert to their true faith as soon as it was possible.

Navarre, unaware that his new wife had saved his life, did not trust her and believed that she must have been party to the stratagem. He planned to flee Charles's tyrannical, scheming court and his wife's evil family at the earliest opportunity. This would prove difficult because his position was precarious, and he and Condé were kept under constant surveillance. Many years later, Navarre wrote of the anguish he had felt after so many of his friends, whose safety the king had assured, and to whom Navarre had given his word of honour, had been murdered subsequent to his marriage, many in front of his eyes.

Typically, Catherine's first thoughts were not of the thousands of innocent people who perished, but of herself and how to keep her son on his throne after such carnage. Charles's physical and mental health rapidly deteriorated, which is not surprising since he had lost so many of his great friends in such a horrific manner, and by his own hand. His mood swung from boasting about how he had ordered so many heretics to be killed, to total despair. He blamed his mother for deceiving him into betraying them, and claimed that the screams of the murdered Huguenots kept ringing in his ears.

To boost the public's opinion of Anjou after his despicable part in the massacre of Huguenots, when the last of the hereditary rulers in Poland died without a male heir, Catherine presented Anjou as a candidate. He was duly elected monarch of the Polish-Lithuanian Commonwealth and reigned from September 1573 to 1575. They also gave him the title of Grand Duke of Lithuania.

Now that his brother was removed from court intrigues, and Charles's health was failing, Catherine's youngest son Alençon set *his* sights on an early ascendancy to the throne. He had never had a close relationship with his brothers and had become a *politique* in the hope of securing Flanders when Coligny was preparing for war with Spain. After the admiral's murder, Alençon and Navarre gave a written promise to the Huguenots to exact revenge. The two young men clandestinely formed a party of Catholic and Huguenot nobles, known as the Malcontents.[*]

Since the massacre those who survived became stronger and more determined to fight for equality, and the new Huguenot chiefs recruited a great number of new converts. Many Catholic aristocrats, disgusted at how the royal family had behaved, became moderates and actively conspired against Charles. They disagreed with his policies and fought for more freedom for the Huguenots. Alençon's reasons were less altruistic. He was jealous of the favours bestowed upon his brothers and wanted glory and power for himself. Catherine was aware that her youngest son and Navarre

---

[*] A Malcontent is someone who is dissatisfied with a situation and is prepared for rebellion to change it.

were principal Malcontents and continued to keep them prisoners, albeit in luxury. The Prince de Condé had previously managed to escape and join his allies in the south. With funding from Alençon's admirer Queen Elizabeth and troops from the German princes, negotiated by Condé, the Malcontents eventually became more powerful than the king.

In early 1574 they planned to attack Charles at Saint-Germain-en-Laye. At the same time, they intended to rescue their two leaders from Catherine's tyranny. The queen mother was warned about the plot and fled to Vincennes with the hapless brothers-in-law captive in her carriage. The dying king followed in his litter with the terrified courtiers not far behind. Alençon and Navarre were implicated in the conspiracy against Charles and were kept imprisoned at Château de Vincennes awaiting their fate.

The cowardly Alençon, terrified of being accused of treason, tried to ingratiate himself with his mother by betraying his loyal friends Annibal de Coconas and Joseph Boniface de La Môle, who were collaborators in the abortive attack. La Môle was also accused of making an attempt on the king's life when a wax effigy stuck with needles, obtained from the astrologer Cosimo Ruggieri, was found in his possession. Both men were beheaded for their role in the intrigue, and for conspiring against the king. La Môle was a lover – one of many – of Marguerite. She is said to have been so distraught when he was killed that she embalmed his head and kept it in a jewelled casket. Alençon and Navarre narrowly escaped being beheaded for treason, and were pardoned by Charles, but they were kept at court against their will.

Charles was married to Elisabeth of Austria, with whom he had a daughter. At heart he was not a devout Catholic, and his declared mistress was a beautiful Huguenot, Marie Touchet, who bore him a son in 1573. The king was thrilled and named him Charles de Valois, Duc d'Angoulême, but he did not have long to enjoy his son as he died of tuberculosis, aged twenty-four, the following year at Vincennes. He entrusted the child to the care of his younger brother Anjou, who faithfully fulfilled his obligation.

Catherine was distraught after the king's death and spent an enormous amount of *écus* on his funeral. However, after a short mourning period her grief did not deter her from sending for her *Chers Yeux* Henri as soon as she could. Much to her delight, not long after his coronation at Wawel Cathedral in Poland, Henri and his suite abandoned the Polish throne, and the responsibilities that went with it, and fled. After a leisurely tour of Italy, he and his inner circle returned, their bags stuffed with priceless Polish gems and other items of value, seemingly stolen with Catherine's approval.

An eyewitness account of the St Bartholomew's Day Massacre.
Painting by François Dubois. Oil on panel 94x154cm.
Cantonal Museum of Lausanne.

CHAPTER TWELVE

Henri III, The Last Valois King

Since a ruler can't be generous and show it without putting himself at risk, if he is sensible, he won't mind getting a reputation for meanness.[1]

Niccolò Machiavelli, *The Prince*

Henri d'Anjou, King of Poland, was crowned Henri III of France in February 1575 at Rheims. On ascending the throne, he inherited a bankrupt kingdom with many people in a dire state of poverty. Adding to his problems, the Malcontents were growing in number, wealth, and discontent. He left Catherine to sort out these mundane matters while he rested on his opulent bed, his head propped up on silk pillows lavishly embroidered with fleurs-de-lis. Henri surrounded himself with a circle of frivolous, coquettish, and foppish young noblemen known as *Les Mignons* – The Dainties – who followed him everywhere and treated him like a god. Oblivious to the state of the country's finances he spent a fortune on these favourites, showering them with the most expensive gems, clothes, carriages, and property.

These effeminate young men wore their hair long, and 'crimped and re-crimped in the most artificial way, tucked up beneath their little bonnets of velvet as women of the town wear it and the starched ruffles of their dress shirts half a foot long, so arranged that their heads above them looked like the head of Saint John's on a platter... and they did not do anything except gamble, swear, dance, bow, fight ...'[2]

It was traditional for kings to be seen by their subjects riding through towns and cities on horseback, followed by knights, nobles, and marching soldiers but Henri preferred to hide in a gold, shuttered horse-drawn carriage, gifted by the Viennese. His behaviour, and that of his young devotees, caused great interest and gossip. Unlike his predecessors, although in better health, he was not interested in blood sports or manly pursuits. He preferred the extravagant celebrations of court life, where he could show off his expensive jewels and fine clothes. He wore diamond earrings and strands of pearls, tinted his coiffed hair with violet powder, and wore copious amounts of makeup.

He loved jousts, feasts, and masked balls where he preferred to dress as a woman. When attending the marriage of one of his advisors he 'appeared after supper masked, and at the head of about thirty masked ladies of court. All were dressed in cloth of silver or white silk richly embroidered with pearls and other precious stones. The maskers began to act in such a way that the greater part of the wedding guests and all the "wisest ladies" withdrew and there followed in the presence of the King a very wild scene.'[3]

Henri was married by choice to the beautiful Louise de Lorraine-Vaudémont, who remained childless. He continued to avoid the responsibilities of state affairs, relying on Catherine to advise him as she had done with her other sons. The king was an impassioned Catholic and disliked the Huguenots, but he listened to his mother and was at times surprisingly tolerant towards them. He understood that this was the only way to save his country from total disaster.

Navarre and Alençon continued to be closely watched at court to ensure that neither escaped. Henri was determined to cause conflict between them because in his opinion their subversive activities were becoming a danger to the realm. Thus, he instructed one of his *mignons*, the mincing, coiffed, and spiteful Le Guast, to arrange for the promiscuous Charlotte de Sauve, a member of Catherine's *Escadron Volant*, to seduce them both thereby causing discord. Charlotte, a beautiful, beguiling, married noblewoman, was always happy to spy for Catherine by sleeping with aristocrats regardless of who they were. 'With completely cold detachment she [Catherine] made use of those men who were unable to control their lechery, and those women whom she controlled were completely devoted to her, for they could make love under the pretext of serving the Queen's policies.'[4]

Navarre and Marguerite were estranged, and both continued to sleep with others. Referring to Alençon and her husband, Marguerite observed in her *mémoires*, 'This occasioned such jealousy betwixt them that, though her favours were divided with M. de Guise, Le Guast, De Souvray and others, any one of whom she preferred to the brothers-in-law [Navarre and Alençon], such was the infatuation of these last that each considered the other as his only rival.'[5] This was typical of life in the corridors of power – no one could be trusted.

Henri's plan worked and the two men became alienated. Regardless of their religious differences, Navarre grew closer to Guise and the king, who much preferred his brother-in-law to his younger brother Alençon. 'The situation was so bad that even outsiders knew that the King hated his brother with a deadly hatred... One day they will cut the throats of one another.'[6] Henri's court was a violent and aggressive bear pit of malicious whisperings, sexual innuendo and murder. Best friends could become worst enemies overnight. Navarre, rather boastfully, wrote to a cousin describing the dangers he constantly faced:

The court is the strangest place you ever saw. We are nearly always ready to cut each other's throats. We carry daggers, mail coats and often cuirasses under our clothes... The king is just as much threatened as I am. He loves me more than ever. Monsieur de Guise and Monsieur du Maine never leave me... You never saw how strong I am in friends in this court. I brave all the world. All the cliques which you know about hate me to the death for the love of Alençon and have the third time forbidden my mistress [Charlotte de Sauve] to speak to me and watch her so closely that she would not dare to look at me. I am only waiting the hour to give them battle, because they say they will kill me, and I want to get ahead of them.[7]

Navarre and Alençon soon realised that they had been duped by the king, and that their lives were in danger if they remained. Hence, they renewed their friendship and planned to flee as soon as possible. The latter finally managed to escape his gilded jail in September 1575. His sister Marguerite recalled, 'Accordingly, as soon as it was dusk, and before the King's supper-time, my brother changed his cloak, and concealing the lower part of his face to his nose in it, left the palace, attended by a servant who was little known, and went on foot to the gate of St. Honore, where he found Simier [Alençon's envoy] waiting for him in a coach, borrowed of a lady for the purpose. My brother threw himself into it and went to a house about a quarter of a league out of Paris, where horses were stationed ready.'[8] When Henri discovered that he was missing, he flew into a rage. Furious, he ordered him to be brought back dead or alive. 'He is gone to make war against me; but I will show him what it is to contend with a King of my power,'[9] he snarled. With the help of his allies, Navarre escaped a few days later and joined Alençon, Condé, and their eminent followers in the south, leaving Marguerite at court.

After several attempts Catherine arranged to meet her youngest son in Sens. She hoped to tempt him from the Malcontents' clutches and entice him back before he caused any further problems. Sensing trouble, and knowing how deceitful his mother could be, Alençon arrived accompanied by a retinue of high-born *politiques* and Huguenots, supplemented by six thousand German cavalrymen. After much discussion and shedding of tears, Catherine eventually persuaded her son to disband the Germans and return with her to Saint-Germain-en-Laye, but he drove a hard bargain. In May 1576, he negotiated *La Paix de Monsieur* – The Peace of Monsieur, also known as Edict of Beaulieu. He was granted lands, titles, and his elder brother's former title the Duc d'Anjou – to save confusion I shall continue to refer to him as Alençon. The edict awarded unprecedented privileges to Huguenot nobles, such as the right to practise their religion openly except at court or in Paris. It also awarded them large tracts of land and titles.

Although delighted that his brother was prevented from causing more dissent, Henri was livid with Catherine for conceding the huge privileges given to the Huguenots and was even more determined to start a war against them. He wept with fury as he signed the peace agreement, and his relationship with his mother changed from that day. Fearing repercussions, the queen mother admitted to one of her favourite advisors that she had only agreed to Alençon's terms in order to entice her son back to court, and not to help the Huguenots. Nevertheless, much as she desired to finally destroy them, she was under no illusion as to how influential they now were, and that to declare war on them was not in the interest of the country. Having dispensed with the former Huguenot leaders in the massacre, Catherine now attempted to toady up to the new ones. To placate them she travelled extensively in the south for fruitless peace talks.

The huge concessions ceded to the Huguenots after the Peace of Monsieur, and Catherine's spurious efforts to appease them, further endangered Henri's rule. The intransigent Catholics and the Paris populace were vehemently against the edict. To retaliate, the Guises and their allies started to form alliances and leagues. Tensions were high and the religious divide regressed into open warfare. To convince the Guises that he loathed the Huguenots as much as they did, Henri feigned a friendship with his younger brother, who was as duplicitous as their mother.

When Alençon returned to court Marguerite remembered, 'The King received him very graciously... he turned his thoughts entirely upon the destruction of the Huguenots. To affect this, he strove to engage my brother against them, and thereby make them his enemies...'[10] Flattered by the attention he was getting from Henri,

Alençon wasted no time in joining the royalists and fighting *against* the *politiques* and Huguenots instead of *for* them. In May 1577, under the command of the Duc de Nevers, he captured one of the Huguenot strongholds, La Charité-sur-Loire, and later organised the massacre of Protestants in the town of Issoire in Auvergne. The Huguenots never forgave this odious apostate for his despicable betrayal.

The king still minced around with his bejewelled *mignons*, especially his favourite, the unpopular and malicious Duc d'Épernon, which did not help his cause. It is not known whether Henri practised homosexuality, since his sexual inclinations were discordant with his strong Catholic beliefs. This turmoil created a huge moral conflict for him that caused extreme swings of behaviour. Periods of licentious actions were followed by strict penance. He joined a masochistic order of penitents known as the Flagellant monks and became obsessive in his devotions, beating himself with a chaplet – a wreath made of small skulls – or sitting in a trance-like state of self-mortification and prayer for hours.

Alençon died of tuberculosis in June 1584 at the age of twenty-nine. The death of her youngest son was disastrous for Catherine, as under Salic law only males could ascend the throne. The queen mother's dynastic dream was over. To the delight of the Huguenots, but not the radical Catholics, Navarre became heir presumptive. It was evident by then that the king would die childless.

After the death of Alençon, insurrection escalated as the network of provincial leagues grew and merged with the Catholic League, with Guise and his family in control. Henri was considered unfit to rule by many, and pamphleteers had a field day distributing pamphlets throughout the country. They claimed that the king and the Valois dynasty were execrable, obsolete, and pro-Huguenot. Many Catholics, both nobles and the proletariat, turned against the royal family and some even contemplated replacing them with the Guises. They became subversive activists and engaged in open rebellion to keep Navarre off the throne when the time came.

The League was determined to prevent a Huguenot, especially a member of the House of Bourbon, becoming king, leaving Henri with no alternative but to wage war, but he was unable to fight both Catholics and Huguenots concurrently as both sides possessed stronger armies.

Henri was determined to demonstrate to the League how much he desired to rid France of Protestants, but they did not believe him. Regardless of their religious differences, the king had always respected his courageous, honourable brother-in-law, and viewed Navarre as the rightful heir. In view of this he made a public statement to the Provost of Merchants in support of Navarre, who he expected to convert, but the Huguenot had no intention of deserting his beliefs. Although unquestionably loyal to the king, he was not prepared to abandon his faith. His refusal played into Henri's enemies' hands and started a succession crisis.

By early 1585 the Guises and the Catholic League, with Philip's continued help, had become so powerful and dangerous that the king was forced to backtrack, leaving him no option but to accede to nearly all their demands. The Treaty of Nemours was signed in July by the queen mother and representatives of the House of Guise. In general terms it revoked all previous edicts of pacification including the Peace of Monsieur, and effectively banned Protestantism. Many important Huguenot towns were ceded to the Guises and their adherents, and honours were showered upon them.

Eleven days later Henri was forced to go one step further and sign a *lit de justice*, which officially removed Navarre from succession. It was unconstitutional for a king to bar a legal heir from ascending the throne, and this together with signing the Treaty of Nemours went against all Henri believed in. He was distraught. He had always loathed the charismatic, good-looking Guise, and his frustration and hatred increased.

A pretender was chosen at a clandestine meeting by the League with Philip and the pope's backing. He was the elderly Cardinal de Bourbon – the younger brother of the deceased Antoine and

Condé, and the cardinal Catherine had deceived into agreeing to marry Marguerite and Navarre. The plan was that he would become King Charles X upon Henri's death. Espionage was rampant between England and France, and Queen Elizabeth was warned of the threat to the French king before he was aware of the dangers.

Friendly, flattering letters had always passed between Catherine and Elizabeth, whatever their private feelings towards each other, as both considered the Habsburg Empire a threat to their kingdoms. The formation of the Catholic League, backed by the pope and Philip, left Elizabeth vulnerable. She desperately needed an ally. Since she was also a trusted confidante of Henri, she broke protocol and wrote to warn him of the plot to steal his crown. On receiving her letter, the king kept the pretender hidden by continually moving him from one château to another.

The ensuing conflict is often referred to as the War of the Three Henris, each leader fighting for survival: Henri of Navarre for his right of succession, Henri III to retain his throne, and Henri, Duc de Guise, to usurp them both. In the end all three died by the assassin's knife. Navarre knew that to become king when the time came, it was necessary to win a decisive Huguenot victory over the League. Thus, with the help of the Prince de Condé, the Duc de Damville, and the Duc de Joyeuse, together with *politiques* and sympathetic anti-Guise Catholic nobles, he amassed a substantial army in the south. Meanwhile, Guise was preparing to fight the Huguenots with the blessing of the pope and assistance from Spain. Both armies were much stronger than the royalists.

The king became ever more reclusive and eccentric, and the queen mother's hold over her son was tenuous. He was a loose cannon. Catherine continued travelling the country holding peace talks in an attempt to salvage the critical situation. The execution of Mary, Queen of Scots at Fotheringhay Castle for treason in February 1587 further outraged the Catholics, especially the Guise family to whom she was closely related, thus escalating persecution of Protestants throughout Europe.

Henri was constantly at risk of capture and assassination from Guise supporters, and the Duchesse de Montpensier, sister of Guise and a fanatical Catholic, was behind many of the plots. To protect himself from his enemies, he employed forty-five ruthless killer bodyguards, mainly consisting of lesser nobles from Gascon. The people of Paris became increasingly exasperated with the king's indecisiveness, hesitancy, and failure to defeat the Huguenots. For them there was only one faith and one leader, and that was Guise. He was seen as their sole saviour from Protestantism.

Fearing for their future and that of Guise, the Parisians formed *Les Seize* – Council of Sixteen – after the sixteen quarters of Paris. They conspired to kidnap Henri on 24 April 1588. He was warned of the plot and banned Guise from entering the city, but the rebellious duke ignored the royal interdict. As he rode into Paris, he was greeted by the inhabitants shouting, 'Long live Guise! Liberator of France, pillar of the Church, exterminator of the heretics!'[11]

In an act that dishonoured a privilege of the city of Paris – not to have foreign troops quartered in the city – the desperate king decided to reassert his authority. He recklessly mustered an army, including Swiss mercenaries, to attack the capital. But espionage was prevalent, and the Parisians were warned. On 12 May, on the orders of the League, they defended themselves by barricading the streets with wagons, pieces of timber, and *barriques* – wine barrels – and locked the city gates. The Bastille had capitulated, and Guise took control of the government in what became known as the Day of the Barricades.

The king fled to Chartres with his newly formed bodyguards to fast, pray, and scheme, leaving Catherine to pick up the pieces. Full of hate and fear, and with the knowledge that Guise posed a serious threat to the crown and his life, Henri planned to strike first. His strategy was to kill his adversary on 23 December Guise spies soon learnt of the king's plan, and friends and family repeatedly warned the duke that his life was in great danger, yet he refused to believe that Henri, who in his opinion was a coward, would dare to harm him. How wrong he was.

The court was based at Blois for Christmas and after spending the evening as usual with his mistress, the ever-generous Charlotte de Sauve, in the comfort of her luxurious chamber, the arrogant duke retired to bed still ignoring the desperate warnings given by family, friends, and retainers. On the appointed day, eight of Henri's assassins, led by Bellegarde, were selected to carry out the evil deed; eight more were chosen to prevent the duke escaping, and the rest were hidden around the château. After attending Mass and calmly eating a breakfast of prunes, Guise was summoned to an urgent meeting with the king. As he confidently made his way to the royal chambers, many people stopped to warn him of the danger awaiting him, but he laughed at their fears. After entering the royal anteroom where Henri's councillors were assembled around the open fire, the door of the inner sanctum swung open. Guise entered expecting to see the king but was met by his henchmen who had been hiding behind a tapestry. Before he had time to escape, they fell upon him, plunging their daggers deep into his body, and left him dying at the foot of the king's bed. His brother, Louis, the influential Cardinal de Guise, died on the pikes of his assailants the following day as he attempted to flee from the basement where he had been hiding, and other family members were imprisoned.

Catherine, who was indisposed with a chest infection, knew nothing of her son's plan but she must have heard the commotion as her rooms were located on the floor below. According to her Italian doctor, Dr Cavriana, subsequent to the murder Henri strode into his mother's chamber, and, after enquiring about the state of her health, calmly confessed to the killings. 'Good morning, Madame, I beg you to forgive me, Monsieur de Guise is dead, and no more will be spoken of. I had him killed in order to forestall the same plan that he had formed towards myself. I could no longer tolerate his insolence...' He added, 'I intend now to be the King and no longer a captive and a slave.' Henri ended his speech by declaring that 'he would "wage war" against the Huguenots with ardour, for he intended to extirpate heresy from the realm.'[12] Giovanni Mocenigo, the Venetian ambassador in whom Catherine often confided, claimed that she replied, 'My son, I am pleased to hear it, so long as it be for the good of the State... At least I ardently desire it.'[13]

There was uproar in Paris subsequent to the murder of Guise and his brother, especially among his family. The League wasted no time in declaring war on the king and instituted criminal charges against him. Despite his wish to destroy the Huguenots, to protect himself he had no choice but to combine forces with Navarre. The League, now led by another Guise bother, Charles, Duc de Mayonne, held most of northern and eastern France including the major cities of Rouen, Orléans, Lyon, and Toulouse.

Catherine de Médicis died, at the age of sixty-nine, in the arms of her precious *Chers Yeux* Henri at Blois on 5 January 1589. Her death was probably precipitated by the shock and distress caused by her son's drastic and dangerous actions. It was rumoured that she was poisoned, which is perfectly feasible given the circumstances, but officially she died of pleurisy. Catherine had 'no sooner drawn her last breath than nowhere did they pay more notice to her than to a dead goat.'[14] Many described her as a schemer who did not stop at murder to get her own way.

Much Later, Navarre, despite all he had suffered at Catherine's hands, magnanimously defended her. 'I ask you what a poor woman could do, left by the death of her husband, with five little children on her arms, and two families who were thinking to grasp the crown – ours and the Guises. Was she not compelled to play strange parts to deceive first one and then the other to guard, as she has done, her sons, who have successfully reigned through the wise conduct of that shrewd woman? I am surprised that she never did worse.'[15] Most Huguenots had nothing good to say.

Two days after Catherine's death, 'the Sorbonne proclaimed that it was just and necessary to depose Henri, and that any private citizen was morally free to commit regicide.'[16] Aware that there was a price on his head, Henri joined Navarre and fled with him and their adherents to the royal camp at Saint-Cloud, six miles west of Paris, where they planned revenge. The two kings had many followers and were united by a common cause – to capture Paris and other major towns from the Catholic League. They raised a substantial army, augmented with German troops and Swiss mercenaries. Charles, Duc de Mayonne did not possess his brother's military prowess and lost many of the towns and cities that had been promised to the League.

On 2 August 1589 an ardent Catholic named Jacques Clément, disguised as a priest, requested an audience with the king, claiming that he had a vitally important message from his supporters. Reassured by Clément's clerical vestments, Henri agreed to see him. On getting close enough to whisper the message, Clément produced a dagger from his capacious sleeve and drove it into Henri's stomach, mortally wounding him. Henri died the next day, thereby ending the Valois dynasty that had ruled since 1328. As he lay dying, he formally recognised Navarre as his legitimate heir. The Huguenots were overjoyed. They felt that they had finally emerged out of darkness and into the light of victory.

The Catholic League immediately proclaimed Cardinal de Bourbon King Charles X, but much to their surprise and annoyance he recognised his nephew Navarre as the rightful king. The Parisians, although not happy with the accession of a Huguenot, were delighted by the king's demise. There was much celebration, rejoicing, and shouts of cheer, especially from the Duchesse de Montpensier, sister of Guise, as she rode ecstatically through the streets of Paris.

CHAPTER THIRTEEN

━━◇━■◦■━◇━━━━━◇━━■◦■━◇━━

'Paris Is Well Worth A Mass'

In a day the rich became poor and the poor became rich.[1]

H. M. Baird

T he Huguenots must have been extremely relieved when Henri of Navarre ascended the throne as Henri IV, the first king of the House of Bourbon. He was faced with the almost impossible task of uniting the shattered country and rebuilding the impoverished economy. Initially, he refused to renounce his Protestant faith, and the powerful Catholic League remained sceptical of his sincerity and continued to deny him the right to wear the crown. Hence, he spent the following four and a half years fighting for mastery over his kingdom.

With continued support from Queen Elizabeth and the German princes, Henri's troops defeated Charles, Duc de Mayonne at the Battle of Arques, before sweeping through Normandy and capturing several strategic towns. His main aim was to take Paris, which was no easy task as the citizens thought him a usurper and were prepared to fight to the death rather than accept a Protestant king. Supporters of the Catholic League continued to spread propaganda about atrocities committed against Catholic priests and the laity in England, which did not help his cause.

Henri had to gain the loyalty of the Parisians and the League before he could be accepted as king. This was impossible while he remained a Protestant; therefore, he had no option but to convert. On the advice of his councillors and his declared mistress Gabrielle d'Estrées he eventually capitulated, reputedly with the famous witticism *'Paris vaut bien une Messe'*.[2] He was formally received into the Catholic Church in July 1593 and escorted through the streets by a large procession of priests, clerics, knights, and courtiers to the sacred Basilica of Saint-Denis, where he received forgiveness and publicly participated in the ritual of Mass.

On 27 February 1594 Henri was crowned at Chartres Cathedral rather than Rheims, where coronations were traditionally held, as many Catholic League members continued to oppose him. It did not take long to win the majority of them over and he was formally received in Paris a month later. On the whole Catholics were relieved at the king's apostasy but many Huguenots, especially his close allies, felt betrayed. However, at heart he remained sympathetic to them and marked the end of the Wars of Religion, which had torn the kingdom apart during the second half of the sixteenth century, by signing the important and supposedly irrevocable Edict of Nantes in April 1598.

The edict opened a path for secularism and tolerance. It also granted Huguenots unprecedented rights to worship freely in a church of their choice, as long as it was outside the city boundaries, and they were now openly allowed to record and celebrate important dates. Nevertheless, they were still restricted to certain areas and Catholicism was reaffirmed as the country's established religion. Huguenots gained no exemption from paying the tithe and had to respect Catholic holidays. They also had to obey various restrictions regarding marriage. France was still a kingdom with two religions, one with more rights than the other.

As expected, the edict was bitterly opposed by *parlement* and the High Court of Normandy, who for years refused to obey it, and continued to bend the law to suit themselves and never the Huguenots. The measures designed to protect the latter were continually undermined, and they repeatedly found themselves trapped between two enemies, those in rags on the one hand, and on the other the red-robed judges consisting of clerics and Catholic nobles. Regardless of the malicious judges and the impoverished mobs, 'once the guns had fallen silent' a tenuous harmony prevailed.

Henri's chief minister Maximilien de Béthune managed the state finances, and together they made Paris the great city it is today. They established tree-lined boulevards and constructed buildings, canals, and bridges including completing the famous Pont-Neuf, the oldest bridge across the River Seine which still remains.

Henri's personal life was a different story, as his womanising was legendary. He kept many concurrent mistresses and frequented brothels. When his marriage to the childless Marguerite was finally annulled he married a distant relative of hers, Marie de' Medici, who bore his children including the future king, Louis XIII. Henri was repeatedly unfaithful to Marie and insisted that she raise his many illegitimate children as well as their own. Despite his penchant for many mistresses, he was a popular king as he showed exceptional religious tolerance towards his subjects. Incidentally, he was the inspiration for King Ferdinand of Navarre in William Shakespeare's *Love's Labour's Lost*. To the great detriment of the Huguenots, Henri was assassinated on 14 May 1610 by a fanatic, François Ravaillac, and the days of relative peace ended.

Returning to the Le Plastriers and my ancestor Symon. After the collapse of the family business and the death of their elder brother Jehan in 1567, Symon and his brother Denys eventually followed in his footsteps and became goldsmiths. Traditionally, members swore an oath of obedience to the wardens in the presence of a magistrate and had their name, chosen mark, and date of entry engraved on the copper plaque known as the Table of Copper. Jehan's mark was *Truelle –*

Trowel, Denys chose *Muffle de Lion* — *Mane of a lion*, and Symon opted for *Corbeau* – Crow. It is known that Jehan, the entrepreneur – chapter three – bought a house 'where hangs the sign of a Crowned Crow' in 1476, and I would like to think that was why Symon chose the name.

The Edict of Nantes and Henri's reign had marked the cessation of open hostilities, and many Huguenots prospered. Symon is described in various papers as being *le riche orfèvre* – the rich goldsmith. He married Robine de Moy, daughter of Jehan de Moy and Jacqueline Benye, in 1573 and they lived with their seven children in rue du Gros Horloge. Their second son was my ancestor Jehan II. He and his brother Denys joined the guild in 1600. Jehan chose the mark *Tête de Licorne*, Head of Unicorn, and Denys decided on *Horloge de Sable*, Hourglass.

Goldsmiths became a rich and influential community, many owning other businesses in Paris. They worked with jewellers and dealers in precious stones as well as with clockmakers, who were considered inferior at the time. If my ancestors had known that their descendants became clockmakers after they fled to England, they would not have approved. Some, like Symon, were also merchants and financiers with interests in other friendly countries. It was extremely difficult to become a goldsmith, as the profession was usually passed down from father to son, and the apprenticeship was six to eight years. Contrary to normal practice, the apprentice paid his master and received very little in return other than professional instruction, 'food, bed, housing, fuel and light'.[3]

The number of master craftsmen permitted in the guild at any one time was strictly limited, and it was necessary to pass an examination, pay certain taxes, and acquire an existing business. To achieve the latter, it was customary to marry the daughter or widow of a deceased member, or, more rarely, to buy the goodwill of a business from one who had retired.

Their headquarters were situated in a large house near the St Herbland Church in rue du Gros Horloge, close to Symon's home. The building was presented to the guild by Guillaume Lallemant, who was clerk of the guild. In recognition of his generous gift, he was appointed to the prestigious position of Warden of the Tables,

Stamps, and Marks of the Guild. A century later the conference room of this house contained a bust of Lallemant with the inscription:

Pray God that as a Reward
He gives a House of Heaven
To those who gave one
For our Brothers' use on earth.[4]

As previously mentioned, when visiting Rouen, I was fortunate to see the Table of Copper. It had been hastily prepared to record the names of those registered at the time after hundreds of Huguenots had been murdered when the royalists recaptured the city. The inscription at the top of the plaque reads: 'This Year of Grace 1562, the 26th day of October, this town having been captured and all the equipment of the goldsmiths' houses having been pillaged in accordance with the Orders of the King, it is necessary to make the present list to record the marks of the goldsmiths, as is customary, and to start the same on the 27th day of January 1563 in the presence of the wardens, Charles Dumont, Jacques de Tourny, and Lo Ducloz, for the deceased Guillaume Poullain, and Warden Adam Desrecques, and Pierre Rousell, Clerk of the said register.'[5] There were three hundred members registered at the time.

Jehan, mark of the *Truelle*, was the only Le Plastrier who was a member before the city was besieged, but subsequent ancestors scratched their names on the plaque when they joined at a later date:

Mark	Name	Date of Registration
Truelle	Jehan Le Plastrier	15 January 1560
Muffle de Lion	Denys Le Plastrier	13 November 1571
Corbeau	Symon Le Plastrier	17 December 1568
Tête de Licorne	Jehan Le Plastrier	20 November 1600
Horloge de Sable	Denys Le Plastrier	20 December 1600

Any Tables of Copper that managed to exist during and after the Religious Wars were highly valued and closely guarded by the wardens, who kept them under triple lock and key at all times. A lamb with a crown above is the coat of arms of the city, and always accompanied the goldsmiths' marks.

Symon died, aged seventy, seven days after writing his Last Will and Testament. It is interesting because it demonstrates the strength of the Huguenots' faith, and shows how important family ties were. He guaranteed that all those close to him were provided for and that his brother Denys, who did not have much money, was looked after financially for the rest of his life. He left Denys's daughter, Anne, funds for her trousseau, which she never used as she remained a spinster. He also left a substantial amount to less fortunate Huguenots in Rouen. Symon's Will reads:

Friday, 10ᵗʰ January 1613

May our trust in God who has made Heaven and Earth, Amen! I, Symon Le Plastrier, merchant, living in Rouen, by the Grace of God, sound in mind as well as understanding and recognising that there is nothing more certain than death, and nothing more certain than the hour thereof, at this time hereby announce my Last Will and Testament:

In the first place, I commit my soul to God, my Creator and Heavenly Father, to Jesus Christ, his only well beloved son, who is my advocate, intercessor, intermediary and redeemer, before God the Father; and to the Holy Ghost; praying God to receive it when it shall leave my mortal body, and entreating Him to forgive my transgressions and sins for the sake of His Son, Jesus Christ, who has suffered crucifixion and death for me, and not to take account of my past actions, as I am a poor and miserable sinner. Recognising the Reformed Church in which I have made profession as the true Reformed Catholic and Apostolic Church, which is the spouse of our Lord Jesus Christ and in which rests all my Faith and my salvation, and praying to God to have compassion on me, I entreat my wife and children to live and die in that faith.

So far as regards the worldly goods which God has given me. I wish, desire and intend to divide them into three equal shares, one share for my wife, one share for my children and the third for myself, to be disposed of according to my own wishes. From which latter share it is my desire and intent that the sum of 175 livres shall be given and delivered eight days after my decease to the poor of the Reformed Religion which I profess. Further, I give and leave to my brother, Denys Le Plastrier, the sum of 300 livres, which shall be given to him by my two sons as follows: each month, the sum of six livres, to aid in his support during his life, up to and including the sum of 300 livres; and in case the said brother should depart this life before the total of 300 livres be expended, the remainder shall go to my two sons. Further I give and bequeath to my niece Anne Le Plastrier, his daughter, the sum of 150 livres to promote her marriage, to wit, one third to be expended for her trousseau and the remainder in ready money, provided always she marries with the consent of her father, mother, friends and relatives, in which event the said sum of money shall be handed over three days before her marriage and no sooner. I bequeath 100 livres to Anne Lerbier [a servant] to be given to her by my wife fifteen days after my decease.

I desire and direct that my two daughters, Elizabeth Le Plastrier and Madeline Le Plastrier, shall each have 1,800 livres, a total of 3,600 livres, for their share of my estate and that they shall not ask for more in the division of my property between their brothers. I further direct that the interest of the above 3,600 livres shall be devoted to their support and maintenance with no diminution of the principle: my wife shall be trustee for half of the said principle and my two sons, trustees for the other half of the sum.

I leave and bequeath to my son, Jehan Le Plastrier 1,260 livres, having already given a like sum to my other son Denys Le Plastrier when he went into business. I also give to my said son Jehan Le Plastrier 1,260 livres, being the profit coming to him since he has been associated with me in business as shown by my books, these aforesaid amounts to be handed over before my estate is divided. Further, I desire that my wife should take her third share of my furniture and personal property under the provision of the Costume de Normandie [Norman Code] to leave *outright to my wife, her bed, bedclothes, canopy and other personal effects without diminution of her rights in the rest of my personal property. I appoint her guardian of my two daughters and executrix of this my last Will and Testament.*[6]

His other two surviving daughters Marie and Suzanne are not mentioned, as they had already been provided with dowries when they married. Suzanne and her husband, Pierre Saunier, later died of the plague.

Symon had been a pastor of the magnificent Quevilly Temple, an esteemed yet dangerous position. It was the largest Huguenot church in Rouen, located roughly three hundred metres from the Hôtel de Ville of Grand-Quevilly, marginally outside the city as stipulated by the Edict of Nantes. The temple was an extraordinarily beautiful architectural masterpiece, designed by the architect Gigouday and completed in 1601. It was constructed with twelve sides and built almost entirely from timber with some brick infilling. It was lit by sixty windows, of which there were two pairs in a dormer for each of the sides. A lantern surmounted the roof, enclosing a bell, which was in turn surrounded by fleurs-de-lis, a touching but futile symbol of loyalty to the king. The interior featured two balconies measuring fifty-four feet in diameter, one superimposed above the other, extending round a central space holding pews along the twelve sides. This enabled worshippers to focus on the pulpit and the pastor. Huguenots regularly clustered in the area around the temple, which housed the all-important consistory, library, booksellers, printers, and a college. The latter was the only Huguenot establishment of its kind in Normandy.

It is said, but hard to imagine, that the temple could hold more than four thousand people. It is thanks to a famous architect Nicolas de Genevois that drawings of this exquisite edifice exist today. He took steps to ensure that the plans created by his predecessor were kept in safety to serve as a model for future generations with the words: 'For those who may wish to erect a building for the purpose of a church, wherever they might be able to gather in the future.'[7]

I doubt if anyone since had the expertise or patience to reproduce this wonderful structure. Nicolas de Genevois lived in Rouen and was one of the many Huguenots murdered when Louis XIV revoked the Edict or Nantes, and the irreplaceable temple was destroyed by Catholic mobs. It is commemorated by a delightful, tranquil garden called *La Prêche*, which roughly translated means The Prayer and marks the spot where the temple once stood.

Table of Copper, 1562

*Le Gros Horloge, and archway leading through to 23 rue du Gros Horloge,
photograph taken in 2018*

Original road sign, photograph taken in 2018

A drawing of 23 rue du Gros Horloge, the ancestral home of the Le Plastriers, bought by Jean Le Plastrier in 1662

A similar 17th century house to the Le Plastrier home, showing the rear of the property

Upper part of 23 rue du Gros Horloge [middle building in green]. Photo taken in 1984.

Architect's drawing of the Quevilly Temple, Rouen, 1661

CHAPTER FOURTEEN

Hopes Dashed

Blood flowed in every part of the kingdom.[1]

H. M. Baird

J ehan II, *Tête de Licorne*, son of Symon and Robine, inherited
his father's successful business as stated in his Will, and was
a master goldsmith. He married Ester Cossart, daughter of
Jacques Cossart and Marguerite Toustain. They also lived in rue du
Gros Horloge with their two surviving children Ester and Jean. Ester
was widowed shortly after her son's birth, but fortunately received a
sizeable inheritance from her late husband and was wealthy in her
own right. She later met and married Abraham Du Pont, with whom
she had a son.

Jean became an elder of the Quevilly Temple, and a merchant
and financier with contacts in many countries. He owned a house in
the city centre, and in 1656 purchased Proche le Moulin, in Lacroix-
Saint-Ouen from Isaac Papavoine. Six years later he bought 23 Rue
du Gros Horloge from Pierre de la Mare. His first wife was Rachel
Le Bon, with whom he fathered five children. Like so many women

at the time she died during childbirth in 1648. The following year he married Rachel Du Garde, who was also descended from a family of goldsmiths, and was a childhood friend. They had four daughters and one son, my ancestor Robert.

I have often wondered how the Le Plastriers endured the persecution and fighting that occurred during the Wars of Religion, and later, much of it in Rouen. It would be especially interesting to know how they survived the siege of 1562 when goldsmiths were the first to be targeted. Regardless of the constant threat and danger of massacres and wars, in times of peace many Huguenots prospered and led a privileged life. They owned large, expensive, and elegantly furnished homes, yet lived and dressed simply. Being highly religious, they spent much time worshipping at the Quevilly Temple, subsequent to its completion in 1601, and helping the less fortunate, of which there were many. Protestantism was often seen as a narrow interpretation of the scriptures, with work, charity, and piety regarded as virtues. The years of persecution had created a cell-like structure of congregations, consistories, and synods where Huguenots united in matters of both religion and business. Wealthy merchants became almost as powerful as lesser nobles, and doubtless had many influential friends.

After several years of blessed relative peace and tranquillity following the Edict of Nantes, the Le Plastriers lived through the traumatic years of Louis XIII and his son's tyrannical reigns. Louis was nearly nine years old when he succeeded his father, Henri, and became king of France and Navarre. His mother, Marie de' Medici, acted as his regent, but she was as devious and ambitious as Catherine had been and immensely unpopular. She surrounded herself with Italian courtiers with whom she endlessly plotted and schemed, which led Louis to seize power in 1617, and take the drastic step of exiling her, and executing her Italian retainers including the influential Concino Concini.

The king was taciturn, distrustful, and weak. He relied heavily throughout his reign upon his shrewd and conniving chief minister,

Cardinal Richelieu, known as *l'Éminence Rouge* – due to the red robes he always wore. Louis practised and believed in the divine right of kings, which meant that he had absolute power with no meddling from the nobility or the church. He and Richelieu used many strategies to strip the aristocracy of the power they had always held over the monarchy. One was to demolish their fortified castles so that they could not be used as places in which to plot against the king.

Louis married Anne of Austria,* sister of Philip IV of Spain, thus cementing a political and military alliance between the two countries. She was betrothed to Louis at the age of eleven, and married at the age of fourteen, but the marriage was not a happy one. After twenty-three years of stillbirths, the future Louis XIV was born in September 1638 followed by his brother Philippe d'Orléans two years later. Anne idolised Louis, and constantly reminded him that he was anointed by God and blessed by the sun. Hence, he wallowed in self-glorification for the rest of his life.

She agreed with Richelieu and her husband's uncompromising approach towards the Huguenots but, being Spanish, she did not concur with Richelieu's opposition to the Habsburg dynasty. He accused her of sending military secrets and information to her brother Philip and, after being mercilessly interrogated, she was kept under house arrest for a number of years. Anne was very beautiful, and had many admirers including the George Villiers, Duke of Buckingham. She is one of the central figures in Alexandre Dumas's novel, *The Three Musketeers*.

Tensions had been growing steadily more severe as the Huguenots continued to gain influence and wealth after the Edict of Nantes. Catholics were concerned that they were plotting to overthrow the kingdom, hence the smouldering hatred flared up again with renewed attempts from many quarters to persuade them to convert. Richelieu, although mindful of their standing, detested them, and, regardless of

---

* Despite her Spanish birth, Anne was known as Anne of Austria because the rulers of Spain were members of a senior branch of the House of Austria.

the Edict of Nantes, it was not long before repression of Huguenots escalated.

They were once again forbidden to conduct religious ceremonies or attend their places of worship. Iron-barred castle dungeons were turned into prisons and convents in which to incarcerate women of all ages. These poor souls were mainly the wives of law-abiding, upstanding merchants. If they weren't dead within a few weeks they could remain imprisoned for years, half-starved, beaten, and continually raped. Men were arrested and condemned to the notorious galleys.

The king, who had assembled a formidable army, decided to finally eradicate the Huguenots by systematically capturing their strongholds. On hearing of his plan many fled to their safest bastion La Rochelle, which was still virtually under independent governance. The new leaders Henri de Rohan and his brother Soubise organised a rebellion to defend their citadel, which motivated Richelieu to lay siege to the port in 1627.

Charles I of England, married to Louis's sister, the devout Catholic Henrietta Maria, reluctantly agreed to support the Huguenots in defending their stronghold. He sent a fleet of eighty ships and six thousand men under the command of the Duke of Buckingham. Unfortunately, the English Navy was not strong enough to withstand the French and retreated after three months, leaving the people to their fate. In August, the royal forces consisting of seven thousand soldiers with six hundred horses and twenty-four cannons led by Charles d' Angouléme – illegitimate son of Charles IX – laid siege to the port.

The garrison was soon reduced to a state of desperate famine, but the citizens refused to capitulate. The Duchesse de Rohan and her daughter valiantly attempted to set an example by restricting themselves to a small slice of horse meat and a piece of bread between them, but it was too late. The people slowly starved to death having eventually exhausted the supply of vermin, dogs, cats, and weeds. In desperation those who survived fearlessly emerged from the relative safety of the fortified city walls and threw themselves upon the king's mercy.

They did not, however, understand the vindictive nature of Louis; who, exasperated by the refusal of the city to surrender, immediately issued an order that the men be stripped naked, and the women denuded to their undergarment, and afterward flogged back to the walls from whence they had just emerged; a command which was so effectually obeyed, that the unfortunates found themselves once more at the gate of the besieged city, sinking from famine, perishing with cold, and wounded and bleeding from the blows they had received, only to be refused readmission to the wretched haven they had abandoned. In this condition they remained during three days and nights; but, eventually, the gate was flung open, and they were permitted again to share the misery of their fellow-sufferers.[2]

The inhabitants resisted for fourteen months, skeletal men and women fighting alongside each other. The besieged city finally fell on 28 October 1628 and became isolated from the world. The population of twenty-seven thousand was reduced to five thousand. This defeat was the final undoing of the Huguenots and was considered a huge victory for Louis and Richelieu, but they are remembered for leaving the country in a critical financial state and for attempting to diminish the disruptive power of the nobility. Equally, they are remembered for their unspeakable brutality towards the Huguenots.

Louis died in May 1643, having stated in his Last Will and Testament that he did not wish Anne to act as regent to the young dauphin, but she had other ideas and persuaded *parlement* to revoke the Will and allow her to govern on behalf of her son. She entrusted the administration of the country to her chief minister Cardinal Mazarin, who was a *protégé* of her nemesis Richelieu. Regrettably, Anne was also an enemy of the Huguenots. When the clergy congratulated her on her regency, she announced that she wished all concessions issued in favour of the Huguenots in the Edict of Nantes to be abolished immediately. Needless to say, they continued to be appallingly violated during her regency.

Hatred felt for Huguenots in Rouen and surrounding areas was demonstrated when the plague killed hundreds, including the only Catholic plague doctor by the name of Bance. There were very few practitioners who were prepared to brave attending an outbreak of the Black Death, and the only one willing to risk his life was a Protestant, but the government refused to consider him. Instead, they instructed the College of Medicine in Paris to find a Catholic. A replacement was eventually found, but in the meantime the plague continued its ravages. Doctors tried strange remedies such as ten-year-old treacle or cutting up dead snakes and pigeons to put on the infected areas. Some thought that sitting next to a sewer or open fire might help to draw the infection out of the body, but there was no cure. Doctors must have looked terrifying dressed all in black with beak-like masks covering their faces.

The grim fourteenth-century, two-storey, cloistered charnel house, adjacent to the magnificent church in Saint-Maclou, was where the dead were placed. Bodies were unceremoniously dumped one on top of the other in the courtyard, which was used as a temporary cemetery until the bones were in a suitable condition to be moved to the ossuary on the second floor. The building was constructed from wooden beams and stoneware, carved with the *Danse Macabre* – symbols of death depicting skeletal faces, gravediggers, and skulls and crossbones. It was originally built during the first plague of 1348 when Rouen lost over half its population. Much later, St Jean-Baptiste de La Salle, founder of the Brothers of Christian Schools, established a school for underprivileged boys in this building.

CHAPTER FIFTEEN

◇━━◈━ ━◆━ ━◈━━◇

The Revocation Of
The Edict Of Nantes

*A juncture had been reached at which the persecution of the
Huguenots could not stand still; it must either advance or
recede.*[1]

H. M. Baird

A nne and Cardinal Mazarin continued to hold the reins of power until his death in 1661, after which Louis assumed the governing of the country. Anne and Mazarin had maintained the concept of the divine right of kings, and Louis resolved to persist with this policy and finally eliminate any remnants of feudalism. He knew how powerful the nobility and clergy were, and that they would continually plot against him unless he gained absolute control. Therefore, he continued to follow his parents' example by subtly and slowly stripping them of their power.

He moved the court to Versailles, deep in the countryside, where he painstakingly converted his father's dilapidated hunting lodge into an opulent palace. Initially, the move was not well received since many of the nobility owned properties in Paris and delighted in the gaiety of Parisian life. Whether they liked it or not they had to follow the king wherever he chose to reside, even if it was in the middle of nowhere. Accordingly, they had no option but to move – trapped in a gilded cage – where they continued to scheme against Louis while at the same time fawning over him in the hope of obtaining favours such as loans, properties, and titles.

No expense was spared on building the palace, which eventually boasted hundreds of rooms and apartments to house the many members of the court. In an attempt to prevent them from plotting against him, Louis ensured that his entourage was lavishly and continually entertained with jousts, feasts, pageants, royal tennis, and masked balls. The latter usually developed into licentious revelry lasting all night, when ladies tantalisingly exposed their breasts, if not more, but not their faces – just like the courts of his predecessors.

Louis became ever more confident, almost supremely so, but he was also heartless and cold. When he first ascended the throne he was a popular and powerful monarch, known as Louis the Great and the Sun King. He reigned for over seventy-two years and brought absolute monarchy to its zenith. He was successful in both domestic and foreign affairs and, having inherited an almost bankrupt kingdom, put the country's finances on a firmer footing.

At the beginning of his reign, he was superficially appreciative of the Huguenots' loyalty and success. Unlike his father he never outwardly 'dropped his mask of respect for the Edict of Nantes, which he repeatedly ratified.'[2] In return the Huguenots kept their heads down and were obedient and loyal subjects at all times. Consequently, he famously declared:

> *Our subjects of the Reformed or Protestant Church have given us clear proof of the affection and fidelity [notably in the present circumstances] with which we will rest very satisfied. We wish then that they may be maintained and guarded in the full and complete enjoyment of the Edict of Nantes and the edicts, declarations, decrees, regulations, articles, and*

warrants in their favour, registered in the High Court and notably in the public exercise of their religion in every place where they have been accorded it; notwithstanding all letters and decrees, as well as our council as of the Courts, and other judgments to the contrary; desiring that those contravening our Edicts may be punished and chastised as the disturbers of the public peace.[3]

'Fine words but put not your trust in princes and politicians.'[4] Although the Religious Wars had ostensibly ended, persecution of Huguenots most definitely had not. The king preferred to turn a blind eye to the oppression that was occurring.

France was not currently at war and François-Michel le Tellier, Marquis de Louvois, Secretary of State for War, thoroughly enjoyed inciting the king's restless soldiers to continually persecute Huguenots. As early as 1681 Louvois encouraged René de Marillac to billet *dragonnade*s in the homes of Huguenots in Poitou subjecting the families to unspeakable intimidation in order to coerce them to renounce their faith. Some genuinely signed the abjuration papers, but others feigned conversion before escaping to safer countries. Poitou, where many wealthy Huguenot nobles and merchants lived, was left in ruins. The brutal Marillac was moved on – eventually to Rouen, the home of my ancestors.

Every official, including the clergy and the king, professed ignorance and deliberately avoided any implication of intimidation and violence, which was prevalent throughout the realm. Occasionally, word of an injustice penetrated through the barrier thrown around the king by his close advisors, for which Foucault, the leader of the dragoons, was half-heartedly disciplined. On one occasion the duplicitous Louvois, Foucault's immediate superior, in a semblance of astonishment and concern, wrote to Foucault:

His majesty has been annoyed to learn that a company and a half of dragoons have been quartered upon a woman at Poitiers, in order to compel her to be converted. I have sent you word so often that these acts of violence are not to his Majesty's taste, that I cannot but be greatly astonished that you do not conform to his orders, which have been so often reiterated to you.[5]

On another occasion Louvois reprimanded Foucault, 'If this does not induce you to restrain yourself, I shall be compelled to beg his Majesty to instruct someone else to write you his intentions in whom you have more confidence.'[6] It is not difficult to guess what disparate messages Louvois sent to the intendants in private. When the Edict of Nantes was revoked, Foucault and Louvois were among the first to drop their masks. François de Harlay, the archbishop of Rouen, was another principal instigator in the destruction of the Huguenots.

Before showing his true colours, the archbishop was considered to be a compassionate and moderate cleric, but, despite his godly persona, his private morals were highly suspect. 'The scandals of his fine house at Conflans were matters of public notoriety; nor did the pamphlets of the day spare the names of the abbesses and women of high rank who frequented it.'[7] He was duplicitous in more than one respect; while seemingly sympathetic to the Huguenots, he was kowtowing to the king.

Latterly, Louis became infatuated with Françoise d'Aubigné, also known as the Widow Scarron or Madame de Maintenon. She had been married to the much older comic poet, Paul Scarron, who left her impoverished upon his death. After many years of struggling financially, with the help of her friend Madame de Montespan – Louis's declared mistress – she acquired the responsible position of governess to the king's many illegitimate children; seven from his relationship with Montespan. Within five years, the outwardly retiring and demure Françoise had shrewdly usurped her friend as the king's acknowledged paramour, after Montespan had been implicated in *L'affaire des poisons*.

This affair became a major murder scandal when a midwife Catherine Deshayes Monvoisin, known as *La Voisin*, was arrested in 1679 charged with witchcraft and burned at the stake the following year. Alchemy, fortune telling, divinations, and the selling of aphrodisiacs and poisonous powders – the latter allegedly used to dispose of unwanted spouses or enemies – were popular in the seventeenth century. Before her death La Voisin implicated a number of prominent members of the aristocracy, who were sentenced on charges of witchcraft or poisoning. She also claimed that Madame de Montespan had bought aphrodisiacs and performed a Black Mass* with her in an attempt to keep the king's favour. Montespan was eventually spared by Louis from any charges.

Although baptised Catholic, Françoise had been brought up as a Protestant by her aunt, Madame de Villette. Like so many women who were considered traitors to France, when very young she was sent to a brutal convent. She managed to escape after writing imploringly to her aunt, begging to be rescued. 'Ah Madame and Aunt, you have no conception what a hell this so-called house of God is to me, nor the ill-treatment, harshness, and cruel actions of the women who have been constituted guardians of my body – not my soul, however, for that they cannot reach.'[8]

Notwithstanding her words of commitment to Protestantism, the indoctrination of the convent obviously worked as once her aunt rescued her, she became a staunch Catholic and eventually the king's *éminence grise*. Arguably, Françoise, Louvois, Harlay, and the Jesuits slowly influenced Louis to take drastic and unforgivable action against the Huguenots. Regardless of his statement made in the early part of his reign, on 22 October 1685, while at Fontainebleau, Louis signed the papers revoking the Edict of Nantes that his grandfather had created to protect the Huguenots, with the hypocritical words:

In as much, therefore, as thereby the execution of the Edict of Nantes and everything that has been ordained in the favour of the said Pretended Reformed Religion has become needless, we could have judged that we could do nothing better, in order to blot out entirely the memory of the troubles, confusion, and disasters which the progress of that false religion

---

* A Black Mass is typically a ceremony attended by satanic groups.

occasioned in our realm, and which gave birth to the said Edict of Nantes,
and the particular articles accorded as its sequel, and all that has since
been done in favour of the said religion…[9]

Known as the Revocation of the Edict of Nantes, it was perpetual and irrevocable just as the previous edict was supposed to have been. Louis's justification was that the original one had only ever been provisional! 'Such was the edict of recall, the most famous of all the laws issued by Louis the fourteenth, as untruthful in its treacherous assurances of security to the peaceful Huguenots, as it was mendacious in the premise upon which it rested – a tissue of deceit and falsehood from beginning to end.'[10]

The king ordered his soldiers to demolish all Protestant churches. Huguenots were now forbidden to practise their religion in their homes, or in any other place. Dissenters who refused to embrace the Catholic faith, or were caught trying to escape, had their properties and goods confiscated. Women were murdered or thrown behind the bars of convents or dungeons, and men sent to the horrendous galleys and ultimately to their death. They now had no rights and no protection from their church, and should they attempt to leave the consequences were severe. Ironically, pastors, including some Le Plastriers, were granted a period of fifteen days in which to leave the realm, but were prohibited from taking any possessions or children over seven-years-old with them. Most declined.

The dreaded, uncouth, and illiterate *dragonnades* were now openly sanctioned by the king to enter the homes of all Huguenots, nobles, merchants, and commoners, with orders to force them to sign the documents promising to renounce their Protestant faith. These papers simply stated that 'the undersigned have made the profession of faith above given and abjured the heresy of L'uter [Luther] and Calvin… in order to obey the will of the King.'[11] *Les dés sont jetés* – the die is cast.

The mask was dropped altogether. The demand was instant conversion,
or the dragoons tomorrow. No pretence now of religious conviction.

The mandate has gone forth from Versailles to the commandant of each province. With military precision the order is transmitted by the commandant to his subordinates, by them to the consul of each petty township. Conversion, or abjuration, which was one and the same thing, was a simple matter of direction, as purely mechanical as a drill... Compel all the Protestants that remain to abjure instantly – dans ce moment. In case of non-compliance with the order tell them that they shall have troops quartered upon them tomorrow. Send the troops. See to it that every place be visited within a week, even the last house. [12]

'Persecution was not now to begin; it had long since begun and was raging with fury in various parts of the realm. The edict only made general and uniform the reign of violence that had hitherto been partial and spasmodic and threw the mantle of the law about the lawless acts of iniquity.'[13] Louvois's hatred was limitless. When informed of the obstinacy of the Huguenots in Dieppe, his orders to the intendant Beaupré were:

You are not as regards them [the Huguenots] to keep within the bounds that have been prescribed. You cannot make the maintenance of the troops in their houses too hard and burdensome; that is to say, you should augment the number of men quartered upon them as much as you think is possible to do without relieving the Protestants of Rouen. And instead of twenty sous apiece and their food, you may allow ten times as much to be exacted of them and permit the troopers to commit whatever disorder may be necessary to remove the people from the state in which they are, and to make of them an example that shall be as useful for the conversion of the other Protestants, as their example would be injurious were their obstinacy to go unpunished.[14]

My ancestors continued to worship in the tranquillity of the Quevilly Temple until it was burned to the ground, but they risked having their throats cut every time they hurried through the dark, narrow alleyways where menacing louts were lying in wait. Despite the loss of their sanctuaries and places of worship, and regardless of the increased dangers, the Huguenots' faith remained strong and constant. They gathered in barns or caves – anywhere where they could chant psalms and read the Bible, in the hope of not being discovered. Many brave Catholic sympathisers put themselves in great danger by offering their homes as retreats, resulting in yet more accusations of heresy and subsequent persecutions.

In cities and towns raging vandals were in their element. They took great delight in pillaging Huguenot homes and churches. The lieutenant of Languedoc, referring to the Huguenots, boasted, 'I have this morning condemned seventy-six of these wretches, and hanging them will be quite a refreshment to me.'[15] In many extremist Catholic cities people danced and celebrated when Protestant churches were destroyed, and old men played boules with the heads of dead Huguenots. The stench of burning flesh and the screams of these brave people could be heard all over the country. Not all Catholics were rejoicing, and most were disgusted.

Exasperated by the obstinance of those who refused to convert, Louvois ordered that greater severity should be used to persuade them to sign the abjuration papers. Increased numbers of troops were moved into the homes of the more steadfast, who had not yet converted. These unfortunate families were expected to pay for their upkeep, as well as covering the cost of soldiers living in houses that had been deserted by those who had either fled or been murdered.

The morale of the Huguenots had been severely weakened over the years, and it must have been utterly unbearable for those cultured and genteel people to be subjected to the horrors of enduring unscrupulous men in their homes. As strong as their faith was, many genuinely turned to Catholicism, or found it preferable to cutting social or familial ties. Others converted with their lips, but not with their hearts and signed the papers, while biding time as they plotted ways of escaping to a land of liberty where they could practise their faith without hindrance. Many baptised their children as Catholic to save their lives, planning that once they arrived in their new country they would re-baptise them as Protestant – their children must be saved from the evil path of 'papist idolatry'. No one could doubt the depth of their faith.

Three months after the Revocation, every remaining Huguenot was forced to attend Mass. A decree was also passed stating that all children between five and sixteen were to be removed from parental control at the parents' expense and placed in the care of Catholic friends or relations. If a family were unable to pay for their child's care, they were sent to convents where they were probably starved and beaten by cruel nuns.

In January 1686 a royal ordinance prohibited Protestants and new converts from employing Protestant servants. They were to be thrown out within fifteen days. Male servants were sent to the slave galleys, and females were tossed into dungeons. Many affluent Huguenots escaped with their servants for this reason. The situation can best be described in the writings of Jules Michelet:

The Protestant could stay; one tried to get them to stay. If he would but say one word, he would keep his properties and his homeland, be spared terrible dangers. The émigré of 1793 wished to save his life; that of 1685 wished to keep his conscience. The flight of the Protestants was voluntary. It stood an act of loyalty and sincerity, of horror of lying and respect for one's word. It is glorious for human nature that such a great number of men sacrificed everything in order not to lie, passed from wealth to poverty, risked their life, their family, in venturing such a flight.[16]

CHAPTER SIXTEEN

Braving Escape

Soldiers of the king delighted, the rabble, the idle and thriftless, in other words that part of the populace which is ever on the alert for the opportunities for pillage rather than anxious to secure the rewards of honest industry.[1]

H. M. Baird

On the orders of Louvois, René de Marillac, that cruel man from Poitou, arrived in Rouen in November 1685 and *dragonnage* began in earnest. Apart from nobles, merchants, silversmiths, and goldsmiths, a record of the Protestant bourgeoisie who suffered were: eight hatters, eight drapers, eight dyers, eight skinners, five vinegar makers, four wool-combers, four plasterers, three seedsmen, three shoemakers, three brokers, three clockmakers, and four carpenters. Those who worked in larger industries such as commission agents, linen-drapers, hairdressers, tailors, grocers, woollen-stocking-makers, trunk-makers, and feather-dressers were also recorded. Additionally, there was a single bonnetier, a laundresser, a calenderman, a weaver, a furrier, a cobbler, a tallow chandler, an ivory carver, a carpenter, a druggist, a coiner, and a gravedigger. Not mentioned were a large number of cloth-shearers, practitioners, sugar-makers, and joiners. It is estimated that eight hundred Huguenots in Rouen were persecuted during this time for their beliefs, and at least seventy of them were Le Plastriers.

Huguenots were on the whole peaceful and industrious people, who asked nothing but to enrich their country under protection of the law. They now waited in fear for their doors to be kicked open as their dreaded, unwelcome guests arrived. Once the *dragonnades* were ensconced in their homes they acted like demons; they swore, they tortured, broke windowpanes and tore furnishings apart, raped, and pillaged.

As many as twenty-five of these terrifying men were forced upon a single family. Marillac encouraged the vandals to plunder the Huguenots' elegant homes and to do as they wished with the women and children, resulting in them being thrown into fires or being savagely raped under their own roofs. What panic and anguish mothers must have felt as they watched helplessly while soldiers carried out their wicked deeds; their men powerless to protect them. But their faith was strong, and many refused to sign the abjuration papers.

Obedience to the king's command was the essence of the entire campaign. '*Le Roi le veut!*' '*Le Roi le veut!*' 'The King wills it!' 'The King wills it!'[2] was the cry of the *dragonnades* as they burst, sword in hand, into the houses of the vulnerable and unarmed, demanding the instant conversion of terrified men, women, and children. By 2 November twelve companies of dragoons had been billeted in the homes of Huguenots in Rouen alone, and it was on this date that they were given an ultimatum when Marillac stated:

> *The King's wish is that there be one single religion in his Kingdom; it is a question of Glory of God and the public interest. Diversity of views in matters of faith inevitably leads to a similar result in all civic affairs. It is impossible to subdue this conflict of interests without the re-union of the hearts in one and the same creed, so that animated with but one*

mind they may have in all matters, but one and the same end and aim. Those of you who are willing to return in good faith to the Roman religion, will be treated by His Majesty as his faithful subjects, and by him loaded with benefits. But those who persist in a criminal obstinacy will be considered as rebels against God and the King, and against them we shall be compelled to use expedients which have been granted us to defeat their unhappy stubbornness, to billet troops upon them until they renounce their errors. It is not intended to compel you to make this change in a moment. It will suffice that you sign a declaration undertaking to make your abjuration before Christmas, and you will be given until 2 o'clock this afternoon to make that declaration...[3]

They were given two hours to betray their faith, and make a declaration promising to sign the papers converting to Catholicism before Christmas or suffer unthinkable consequences. Understandably, under extreme duress, many rushed to sign the declaration at the Town Hall hoping to buy time while deciding what action to take. Parents now had to make the most important decision of their lives – and afterlives – to flee or not to flee.

Some decided to genuinely convert, while others remained as clandestine Protestants. My ancestors chose to save their souls and flee. This meant leaving their homeland, sacrificing their homes and businesses, and usually surrendering wealth for poverty. More importantly they risked breaking up the family because it was considered dangerous to attempt an escape *en famille*, especially with young children and infants. Difficult as it is to imagine, many parents put their own spiritual needs before their children and chose to leave them behind to be brought up by Catholic friends or newly converted relatives. They often left long heart-rending written accounts for their children explaining why they had made their difficult decision. They hoped that they would be reunited one day; often they never were.

The true feelings of Protestants forced to sign the papers, pledging to become Catholics against their will, are shown in the famed writing of Isaac Dumont de Bostaquet, a Huguenot from Normandy. He tells us that his courage failed him when he heard the command given, in the presence of the Marquis de Beaupré and Monsieur de Tierceville, to quarter twenty-five *dragonnades* upon him:

> *I confess to my shame and with extreme grief – and I ask God's pardon as long as I live – that I could not resist the order given in my presence to billet twenty-five ruffians in my house. The fear of seeing so many women and girls exposed to the insolence of the soldiers, to whom everything is permitted, compels me to sign before these men [as hideous as demons, and as full of malice and cruelty] a promise, bowing to the King's Will to embrace the Catholic religion before Christmas. That the time was still distant, and I hoped that God would have pity for our misery, and that perhaps things would change by then.*[4]

Symon and Robine's granddaughter Elizabeth Roger, the daughter of their eldest son Denys, mentioned in Symon's Will in chapter thirteen, and two of their great-grandsons Denys and Symon are documented as having soldiers billeted in their homes. Elizabeth, a widow aged seventy-six, was subjected to lodging nine cavalrymen, a commander and five of his aides. After being persistently persecuted she eventually succumbed and signed the recantation papers, but the authorities did not believe that she had genuinely converted, and she had soldiers billeted in her home yet again.

She eventually managed to disappear and was noted in official documents as being 'absent'. It is thought that she escaped to Amsterdam with some of her children, but eventually returned to Rouen where she lived until her death at ninety-six. Elizabeth's daughter Suzanne was not so lucky. Her husband, John Congnard, a tapestry maker, was discovered hiding in Paris and imprisoned. The authorities sold all the family's assets and Suzanne, John, and their children were never heard of again.

Denys Le Plastrier, a merchant, lived in rue des Carmes with his wife, Anne Bocquet, and their five children aged between sixteen and twenty-five. They must have been extremely courageous and stubborn as they had soldiers billeted on them four times. Denys ultimately had his spirit broken, and he and his family were forced to sign the papers promising apostasy. Even this did not satisfy the authorities and all their estates were seized. Disregarding the dangers, Denys and Anne remained, possibly practising their true faith in secret. Their eldest son, also called Denys, who lived in Rue aux Ours close to Notre-Dame, only had one soldier billeted with him – he was lucky. He abjured at the Town Hall in December and, after abandoning his house, fled to Amsterdam. At some stage he returned and died in 1724 while living with his parents. Their other children also escaped to Amsterdam, where they remained.

One of the more distressing stories is that of Denys's brother Symon, his wife, Marie Vereul, and their two daughters, thirteen-year-old Catherine and one-year-old Judith. The family were forced to lodge and feed eight footmen, a captain of cuirassiers, and four cavalrymen as well as their horses. They were brutally abused and violated by the soldiers until, under extreme distress, they eventually capitulated and recanted. The family then went into hiding while planning their flight to freedom.

However thoroughly Huguenots organised their escape, or how much they spent, they were at great risk of being caught and murdered. With this in mind, Symon and Marie made the difficult decision to leave Judith behind in the care of friends. This must have been particularly hard, as they had already lost six children in infancy. Symon was affluent enough to hire a small German boat to take them to Holland, but tragically they never reached their destination. It is recorded that the family died at sea, probably by having their throats cut. They no doubt attempted to smuggle jewellery and gold out with them and were killed by the master or his crew. Women frequently took the risk of sewing valuables in the seams of their underclothes, in the hope of fleeing into the unknown with some form of security. Judith presumably remained in France but was never heard of again.

All Symon's properties and possessions were seized following his unsuccessful attempted escape and Marillac ordered Clinchard, the assistant major of the dragoons, to make an inventory of the family's furniture and other assets. Their house, Maison Amail, on the corner of Grand-Pont and Place de la Cathédrale, is well documented and mentioned in several historical records as being 'known to all Rouen,'[5] probably because it was particularly large and impressive. When Symon and his family lived there it bore a curious sign, *Le mouton qui fait la barbe au loup* which roughly translated means, The sheep shaving the wolf. All signs had a meaning to their owners, and this possibly referred to some ancestor who was a wool merchant.

Some leading merchants, feeling the storm approach, had made arrangements to remove their businesses to other lands. Jean and his sons, Symon, Jean, and my ancestor Robert were among them. They had many influential friends and were fortuitously 'tipped off' that the king was about to revoke the Edict of Nantes. Being forewarned, they planned to move some of the family assets to other countries before the inevitable happened. Undeterred by the dangers, seventy-one-year-old Jean managed to escape to England just before the Revocation, having persuaded the authorities that he had died.

Meanwhile, Robert was confronting his own personal tragedy. His wife of less than a year, Anne Cossart, died after giving birth to Elizabeth at the end of 1684, leaving him with the responsibility of caring for their newborn daughter. How vulnerable and frightened Anne must have felt while carrying a child during those uncertain times. It is to be hoped that her death was not at the hands of the *dragonnades*. Robert was so concerned for the safety of his daughter, when even infants were not spared the horrors that were occurring, that he had her baptised Catholic and entrusted her to friends. As far as we know he did not suffer the indignity of having murderous soldiers living in his beautiful home after Anne died, probably because he was a widower living alone with no wife or children to torment and rape. He abjured at the Town Hall before Christmas, as ordered, while planning his escape to England to join his father. His siblings and mother, Rachel, all made plans to flee separately.

Desperate Huguenots covertly sought ways of leaving, either by sea to England and the Channel Islands, or by land to the Netherlands, Switzerland, or parts of Germany. Both options were extremely dangerous as ports and roads were closely guarded at all times. Apart from the twelve companies of soldiers billeted in the Huguenots' homes in Rouen, a further twenty-four companies were spread out along the coast. Many ingenious stratagems were used, and escapees were frequently assisted by sympathetic Catholics, or newly converted friends who were eager to help their more courageous compatriots. They often knew of routes and hiding places that fugitives were unaware of.

Some of my ancestors, including the Le Blancs, were among those who chose to flee by land to Holland, taking one of the riskier routes through Flanders. The country's turbulent history produced many useful hiding places such as windmills with hidden rooms, but the crossing was fraught with danger. Fogs and mists were useful, and rivers were made passable by hard winter frosts turning them into roads of ice, helping the exhausted refugees to make their way over the longed-for border.

'Suffice to say, that the most novel disguises were adopted, and the most plausible tales were concocted to throw the wary off their guard.'[6] A known way of escaping for wealthier Huguenots was to dress as Catholic peasants, carrying heavy bundles, trudging by foot, and driving sheep as they made their determined way to safety, accompanied by guides who had been well paid for their hazardous undertaking. 'Delicate women, accustomed to luxury and ease, assumed the garb of menials, bedaubed or stained their skin to simulate the marks of long and arduous toil, lest their faces and hands should betray them, and passed the frontiers unheeded, so well did they play their part.'[7]

If escaping by sea, a method used by more affluent Huguenots was to bribe a sympathetic or avaricious captain of a ship. Shipmasters were forbidden under the strictest penalties to assist them. Nevertheless, many mariners were tempted to take huge risks in order to make enormous financial gains. If successful, the Huguenots travelled disguised as members of the crew. This left them at the mercy of the sailors, and it did not take long for the authorities to become aware of this subterfuge. The boats to which many less fortunate refugees were compelled to entrust themselves were often inconceivably small, flimsy craft that could not stand up to rough seas. Many sank, taking the fugitives with them. Some boatmen were accused of purposely drowning unsuspecting and trusting Huguenots, in order to steal items of value saved from their precious possessions. Poorer folk often hid in crates on larger vessels. This was equally dangerous, as the government regularly fumigated the crates with poisonous gas in order to asphyxiate stowaways. 'It was no rare thing for a child to be placed in an empty wine cask and shipped to one of the Channel Isles or to England.'[8]

Many of the sufferers, particularly those who ultimately made good their escape to foreign lands, but some also of those who continued to languish in prisons, convents, or aboard the galleys, wrote graphic and horrifying accounts of their own experience and the experiences of their immediate friends. These manuscripts, some of which still exist, bear every mark of authenticity, and are now reverently preserved by their families.[9]

After having been subjected to the horrors of having soldiers living in their home, Rachel and two of their adult daughters Catherine and Anne recanted at the Town Hall before fleeing to join Jean in England. When Rachel absconded, she was listed as 'missing' from 23 rue du Gros Horloge. The government seized the family's three properties – the house Rachel was listed as missing from, their country estate in the parish of Lacroix-Saint-Ouen, and another property in the city centre. Although my ancestors were lucky enough to salvage some funds and maintain their overseas contacts, they left their homeland, friends, properties, businesses, and most importantly family. In Robert's case his precious child, Elizabeth.

Abandoned possessions were put under state control, before often being given to relatives who had genuinely revoked their faith and remained in France. This happened to Jean and Rachel. Their three properties were granted to Jean's cousin Marie Le Plastrier and her husband, Robert Du Garde, who were probably much less wealthy and therefore extremely happy to become the unexpected beneficiaries.

Regrettably greed for properties and riches often tore families apart during this period.

Unfortunately, there is no documentation as to how my ancestors managed to flee, but we can be certain that it was under extremely harrowing and hazardous circumstances. Huguenots never divulged the means of their escape, or the names of those who had assisted them, to anyone for fear of reprisals from the military.

Within the course of a few years the population of Rouen had shrunk from eighty thousand to sixty thousand. Foreign trade hardly existed, and most workmen and their skilled operatives had emigrated, leaving thousands of properties deserted.

The continuity of life for the Le Plastriers, which had existed for almost four hundred years, ended after this unjustified enforced flight caused by Louis XIV. They were uprooted from all they had ever known and compelled to start a new life in England or Holland. Later they were scattered as far afield as Australia, the West Indies, America, and Africa.

PART TWO

England 1685–1872

CHAPTER ONE

Freedom

*It has been well said that it would be hard to overstate
the importance of the French contingent in the Prince of
Orange's little army of fifteen thousand men.*[1]

H. M. Baird

Jean must have been extremely relieved when Rachel eventually
arrived safely in Dover with their traumatised daughters
Catherine and Anne, aged thirty-eight and twenty-three
respectively. Their other two daughters Marie and Judith, and sons
Symon, Jean, and Robert arrived later, but there is no record of Rachel
and Jacob, two of Jean's children by his first wife Rachel Le Bon. Both
Marie and Anne married Huguenots; Marie to Jacques Hallé from
Calais and Anne to a widower, Nicolas Lefèvre. Judith and Catherine
never married.

Rachel, Catherine, and Anne were naturalised in 1687, which
gave them full citizens' rights. On the whole Huguenots were slow
to acquire naturalisation. They hoped that the religious problems in
France would soon be resolved, and that they would be allowed to
return, reclaim their properties, and reunite with family and friends.

Jean lived happily in London until his death at the great age of eighty-nine, leaving a fortune to members of his family and to the French Church in Threadneedle Street. Rachel died aged fifty-nine not long after arriving in England, which is not surprising considering the anguish and fear she must have endured before and during the dangerous escape with her daughters.

Most Huguenots arrived shivering and terrified, with nothing but the clothes they stood in and little idea of what the future held. Some bravely smuggled their bibles out, hidden in large loaves of bread, and in other ingenious ways. Others, desperate to make a living, brought gold and silver working tools. Buoyed up by their religious beliefs they must have felt huge relief on finding themselves safely on English soil. It was extremely challenging for them, as most had few or no resources and did not speak the language. However, the people greeted them with kindness and sympathy, despite their dislike of foreigners, especially the French. Anti-Popery was at its peak, and there was widespread disgust at how the Huguenots had been treated. This was matched by fears of what might befall Protestants under King James II.

Relatively few Huguenots were able to flee as early as my ancestors, due to the dangers of escaping so soon after the Revocation. If England was their chosen destination they arrived during unsettled times because Charles II had recently died, and James II was an ally and cousin of their professed enemy Louis XIV. James, a staunch Catholic ruling a predominantly Protestant country, was not popular. Concerned that his days on the throne were numbered, he attempted to gain support from the Protestants, and to promote his own minority denomination, by issuing his Declaration of Indulgence. This allowed his subjects to practise their chosen religion without incurring penalties, but despite his efforts of appeasement he remained unpopular.

The people expected his eldest daughter Mary, a Protestant, and her husband, William, Prince of Orange, to succeed him when the time came. This assumption was thrown into disarray when in February 1688 the queen, Marie of Modena, produced a son, James

Francis Edward Stuart. The birth was largely greeted with dismay and disbelief as it came five years after Mary's last stillbirth pregnancy. There were rumours, probably disseminated by James's opponents, that an imposter newborn had been brought into St James's Palace in a copper warming pan and exchanged for Mary's dead infant.

The birth of a Catholic male heir forced James's enemies into action. They wrote to William without delay 'inviting' him to invade England as soon as possible. Thus, on 22 October of that year Huguenots who fled to Holland after the Revocation fought alongside William, who successfully occupied the country the following month. This led to the overthrow of James in what is famously known as The Glorious Revolution. He fled with the queen and his 'warming pan' baby to France the following year, where he was affectionally welcomed by Louis. Parliament confirmed William king, and he and his wife ascended the throne jointly as William III and Mary II. They were respected by their subjects, especially the Huguenots who they supported in many ways. Mary died in 1694 and William reigned successfully until his death eight years later. As they were childless, Mary's Protestant sister Anne succeeded William.

It did not take long for the highly skilled Huguenots to become accepted as they were friendly, chic, resilient, hard-working, and talented. Artisans tended to settle in the narrow streets of Spitalfields, where wooden spools can now be seen indicating where many once lived, while merchants and nobles preferred to live in Westminster. They soon surmounted their appalling difficulties and developed thriving businesses such as silk weaving, lacemaking, clockmaking, and cabinetmaking.

Others brought their expertise in banking and law, and some like my ancestors used their connections to continue trading internationally. They formed a close network with other Huguenots, some previously known to them, others not, but all had suffered persecution. Their unfamiliar diet, foreign language, and religiosity set them apart from other citizens, but they were respected for their integrity, high principles and industry.

There were twenty-three Protestant churches in the area when my ancestors arrived, as Edward VI granted all early Protestants freedom of worship by Royal Charter in 1550. French Protestants arrived as early as 1540 after the Edict of Fontainebleau signed by François I, and others came after the St Bartholomew's Day Massacre in 1572. By 1669 the industrious Protestants had re-established the *Église Protestante Française de Londres* by renovating St Anthony's Hospital Chapel in Threadneedle Street, which had been one of the original Protestant churches before being badly damaged in the Great Fire. Jean and his son Robert later became elders of this church, which was demolished in 1841 to make way for the Royal Exchange. The congregation moved to a site in St Martin's le Grand which was replaced in 1893 with a magnificent building in Soho Square designed by Aston Webb. This grade II listed building, The French Protestant Church of London, is the last remaining Huguenot church in the city.

Protestants who fled for religious reasons are known as *réfugiés*, whereas those who escaped on political grounds at the time of the French Revolution in 1789 are referred to as *émigrés*. The French Hospital was founded in 1718 in Finsbury to improve the welfare of the many impoverished French people and was affectionately known as *La Providence*. It is now located in Rochester where it provides sheltered housing for elderly people of Huguenot descent.

The Goldsmiths' Company was vigilant in protecting their members and foreigners were not allowed to practise. As a result, some Huguenots started businesses outside the city perimeters where regulations did not apply. However, in 1725 the Attorney General announced that the right of entering a maker's mark at Goldsmiths' Hall could not be denied to anyone, whether he was a freeman of the Company or not. Therefore, London guild members had no alternative but to accept foreign craftsmen. French goldsmiths were renowned for their outstanding work, and ultimately gave the trade an important boost both in technical and design skills.

London must have seemed like paradise, despite the fact that it was still recovering from the Great Fire of 1666, during which more than eighty-five per cent of the city was destroyed. New buildings had been hastily erected using shoddy materials, twisting in a haphazard manner along either side of the filthy, cobbled streets and alleyways. Sanitation was rudimentary, and the overflowing cesspit privies were only emptied once a year, leaving many people with no alternative but to empty chamber pots into the Thames or out of windows, slopping the contents into the gutters; Huguenots shouting *garde a l'eau* – watch out for the water. If chamber pots were not accessible ladies of all classes had no option, but to relieve themselves in the nearest corner or where they sat, even when attending royal banquets.

The stench of raw sewage and decaying carcasses was unbearable and unhealthy – no different to towns and cities across the channel. People were wary of drinking water from the murky Thames, and many preferred to share bottles of cheap gin sold by vendors at every street corner. Consequently, there were many drunks, both male and female, staggering about on the streets. The main entertainment came from cockfighting, bear-baiting, and public executions, usually performed in Tyburn and later at Newgate Prison, after which heads were left rotting and hanging from iron posts or gates. The rich paraded in horse-drawn carriages through the stinking, straw-covered streets. Men wore wigs and silver-buckled shoes while women, holding pomanders up to their noses, vied for attention in elaborate gowns. None of them glanced at the poor bystanders, who were lucky if they escaped being sprayed with putrid human waste caused by the heavy metal wheels of carriages, as the horses' hooves slopped through puddles.

Robert Le Plastrier was naturalised in January 1689 and lived in Tower Street. Within a few years he had sufficient powers and means to return to France whenever he wished. This was unheard of when Protestants were still unwelcome, and he was known to be a naturalised Englishman and an elder of the French Church in Threadneedle Street.

He was a trader and financier of international repute, and I quote from an article written by Alice Carter, MA, FR Hist, on The Huguenot Contribution to the Early Years of the Funded Debt,

1694–1714: 'Robert Le Plastrier is an example of a merchant turning dealer. Before 1690, Le Plastrier was, besides being concerned to some extent with loans to the city, a biggish buyer of skins from the Hudson's Bay Company. After that date he seems to turn more and more to finance, appearing in Bank and East India Stock...'[2] While living in Tower Street he married Elizabeth Goulée, a Huguenot who lived in Broad Street, now Broadwick Street in Soho. They had one child, Jean, named after his grandfather. He was baptised in Threadneedle Street, but returned to Rouen with his mother, who died there in 1700.

When Robert fled France after his first wife Anne died giving birth to Elizabeth just before the Revocation, he decided to leave the infant behind to be cared for by Catholic friends. As soon as it was possible, he brought her to England to join the rest of the family. She later married Daniel Pierce in 1711 at All-Hallows-on-the-Wall, reputed to be the oldest church in the city of London, and they had three children: Daniel, Elizabeth, and Elias, who were all born in Cork, Ireland. Daniel senior died in Cork, but it is not known what happened to Elizabeth.

Twice-widowed Robert met and married my ancestor Marie Le Blanc in Amsterdam in 1702. She was the daughter of Abraham Le Blanc and Margaret Vereul – mentioned in the prologue and chapter sixteen. Before the Revocation, they lived in rue des Carmes in central Rouen and owned a country property in Blainville-Crevon, Beaumesnil, but after having ruthless soldiers billeted in their home more than once, they fled to Holland where they became members of the Walloon Church. The Le Blancs were descended from the Royal House of Blois who held a family seat with lands, titles, and estates. Some members of the family were hereditary Barons of Baillieu of Norman Conquest fame, and assisted William the Conqueror in his defeat of England in 1066.

Robert and Marie's four children, Marie, Robert, Louis, and Isaac were all born in London, and I am descended from Isaac. Unlike his father, Jean, Robert never settled in England and the family went back to Rouen in 1709. They all died there apart from Isaac who returned to carry on the Le Plastrier name in England. France suffered hugely after the Huguenots left, which was why Robert, being a financier of world renown, was welcomed back. However, he never recovered the three properties that his parents had abandoned when the family fled to England.

Isaac married a Huguenot, Elizabeth Vealey, of the parish of St Mary Abchurch, in 1732. At the time of their marriage, he was described as a merchant. Not much is known about the family during this period except that they had one surviving son, Jean, or John as he was called now that the family lived in England. He was born in 1735 in Wood Street in the parish of St Albans.

When Isaac and his family lived in London, it was still a city of squalor and stench, but towards the 1700s the elite were able to dispense with chamber pots and invest in water closets, and to buy spring water from private companies. Rich or poor, Londoners alike were a dissolute and louche lot. It is said that one in five women were prostitutes, from lowly streetwalkers to high-class courtesans. Venereal diseases were common, and many people died an agonising death ravaged by syphilis or gonorrhoea. It is comforting to know that Isaac and his family were among the wealthier folk during these appalling and scandalous times and would not have partaken in the debauchery that was so fashionable. With their high Christian principles, neither did they follow the monstrous fashion of owning a black slave-child to dress up to work as a page.

CHAPTER TWO

The Clockmakers

Foreign trade well-nigh ceased, because the master
workmen had emigrated. and their skilled operatives had
followed them in great crowds.[1]

H. M. Baird

I
t is not known what happened to the successful family
business after Isaac died, but their immense wealth had hugely
diminished. His son John is the first Le Plastrier to be recorded
as a chronometer, watch, and clockmaker. Although this venture
flourished, passing down from father to son, it was very different
from being a rich merchant trading all over the world as some of his
ancestors had been. John, or Jean Le Plastrier as he is known in the
Trade Directories, is shown as living and working at 138 High Street,
Shadwell, in the parish of Stepney in East London until he died at
the age of fifty-nine in 1794.

He probably chose Shadwell to sell his wares, as there were
plenty of affluent sea captains and other seafarers to buy his gold
pocket watches and chronometers – the house still stands, and

part of it is now a pub. The port was where many shipmasters, merchants, and explorers owned properties. Captain James Cook, the great British explorer, lived at 126 High Street at the same time.

John married Esther Ball in 1766 at St Dunstan and All Saints Church in Stepney, and their six children, Louis, William, Robert, Suzanne, Elizabeth, and my ancestor Isaac II, were all born and brought up in Shadwell. Pickpockets, prostitutes, and thieves abounded in the port, and John often suffered from thieves trying to steal his timepieces. In May 1786, Benjamin Baker was found guilty at the Old Bailey of stealing a watch. I have quoted the case as it gives a little insight into their family life:

BENJAMIN BAKER: was indicted for feloniously stealing, on the 9th day of May, one watch, with the inside case made of base metal, and the outside made of tortoiseshell, value 20 s, and one seal, value 6 d., the property of John Le Plastrier.

ESTHER LE PLASTRIER SWORN: I lost a watch on Tuesday the 9th of May off my husband's board, close to his vice, between the hours of eight and nine in the evening; I had just lighted a candle, I was in a little room behind the shop; I heard my son cry out, stop thief! And I saw him have hold of the prisoner's coat, with his foot inside the door, one foot within, and one foot without; my son is in his twelfth year; the man wrenched from the child, and the child never quitted him, nor lost sight of him, till a gentleman took him; I did not quit my shop.

ROBERT LE PLASTRIER CALLED: I am in my twelfth year.
Do you know anything about an oath? Yes.
What ought you to do when you are sworn? If I tell a lie, I shall go to a bad place.
Do you know that you are liable to be punished if you tell a lie after you are sworn? Yes.

ROBERT LE PLASTRIER SWORN: I did not see the prisoner come into the shop; I saw the prisoner going to snatch a watch that was hanging in the shop; my father is a watchmaker; I was in the shop standing against the partition. I first heard the chain rattle. I saw the prisoner snatch the watch off the board facing my father's vice; I ran directly, and caught hold of the skirt of his coat, but he, being stronger than me, rushed at me; I pushed him; I was not above a couple of yards from him till he was caught; the watch was never found. I do not know what became of it, I did not see what he did with it; I am sure I saw him take it; I saw nobody else at the door, but the neighbours said there was.

JAMES PAVLIN SWORN: I heard nothing more, than I heard the little boy calling, stop thief! I went down a passage which is opposite my door; I saw a little boy running after the prisoner, and crying terribly; I ran after him, and brought him to the prosecutor's house; the little boy cried out, that is he, that is he; I saw no opportunity of conveying the watch away, except at one turning, and he might be out of sight in a quarter of a minute.

PRISONER'S DEFENCE: I was coming along Shadwell, and this little boy ran out of the shop; he was hollering out, stop thief! I ran after him, and asked him which way he was gone, and he said that way; and I ran, and this man, I believe he is a baker, stopped me; the little boy said, that is not him; and he ran past us; when he came back, he said it was me.

THOMAS BAKER SWORN: I am the prisoner's father; I bred the prisoner up to my own trade, a cooper [maker of barrels and casks]; he is better than fourteen years old, he worked for me till I was lame, and obliged to go to the workhouse; now I am out again; he has not been with me lately, the business has been so slack. What has he been doing? – sometimes one thing, sometimes another; I was not always with him; he behaved always very well at home.
The prisoner called another witness to his character.

GUILTY: To be transported for seven years.

Tried by the first Middlesex Jury before Mr. RECORDER.2

After John's death, his eldest son Louis is shown as a clockmaker working with his son, also called Louis, at 142 High Street, Shadwell. The business was known as Louis Le Plastrier and Son. Louis senior was married to Mary Anne Trappit, and fathered four children. In December 1818 William Smith, aged twenty-one, was found guilty at the Old Bailey of stealing two watches from Louis. I have also quoted this case as it shows the lack of mercy given to thieves, who were obviously poverty stricken, and usually very young:

WILLIAM SMITH was indicted for stealing, on the 28th November, at St Paul's, Shadwell, two watches, value 4 1 the goods of Louis Le Plastrier the elder, and Louis Le Plastrier the younger,

LOUIS LE PLASTRIER: I am a watch and clock maker, and live in High Street, Shadwell, in partnership with my son Louis. On the 28th November, about three o'clock in the afternoon, the prisoner came to our shop, and wanted to look at two or three watches; I took him two or three down. He wished to see two or three more; I handed him three or four more out of the window, one of them he appeared to like very much – it was capped and jewelled – the price was eight guineas. After he had looked at it, he pointed to another in the window, and desired it might be taken down to look at saying, he thought it might do for his mate, if it came to 4 1 or 5 1. He said his ship was going to be paid at the sign of The Cape of Good Hope, in the Commercial-Road, in about an hour, that two or three of his shipmates wanted watches, and he would bring them.

I took the watch down that he pointed at, and before I could put it on the counter with the rest, he pointed at my regular, in a very sharp way, saying, It is not so late as that is it? he hurried out of the shop instantly. I then went to return the watches to the window and missed the capped and jewelled one. I looked again in the window, as I thought it not possible that he had taken it, as I only had my eye off him when I looked at the clock, however, I found it was gone, and another one as well, which I had shown him, worth three guineas. I told my son; he went out one way, and I the other. I went to The Cape of Good Hope public house, but found no ship was going to be paid there. I heard nothing more until Tuesday morning, December 1st when I called on Edwards; he showed me a watch, which I immediately recognised – it was the best watch. He said if I would call at three o'clock, the man who left it would be there. I got an officer from Shadwell Office, and waited there until the prisoner came, we then seized him, and took him into the back room. The officer searched, and found the duplicate of the watch on him, pledged in the Commercial Road for 15 s. – it was not mine. He had got the watch, which he had left with Edwards, as he asked for it when he came. I have only recovered the best watch.

JAMES EDWARDS: I live in the Commercial-Road, near the London docks. On Monday morning, the 30th of November, the prisoner brought me a stop and seconds watch, capped and jewelled. He said it stopped and wanted me to alter it. I said if he would bring it early the next morning, I would do it by three o'clock in the afternoon. He took it away, and brought it again next morning, and said he would call between three and four o'clock in the afternoon for it. Between eleven and twelve o'clock Mr. Le Plastrier came to caution me about a man of colour, who had stolen two watches from him. I asked what sort of watches they were. He said one was stop and seconds, capped and jewelled. I took the watch out of my case and he claimed it. He came again in the afternoon with an officer, and waited for the prisoner, who came. I gave him the watch, and the officer took him.

JOHN BOWN: I am an officer. On the 1st of December, I went with Mr. Le Plastrier to Mr. Edwards. The prisoner came in, and Mr. Edwards delivered him the watch. I took it from him and found the duplicate of another watch on him. I asked him where he lived? He said at Mrs. Axley's at Limehouse. I could find no such person.'

DANIEL CORKER: I live at No. 18 Commercial-Road. On the 30th November, the prisoner came to my shop, and asked the price of a watch. I showed him one, he said he wanted it for a mate, whom he expected in directly – he showed me a watch with Mr. Le Plastrier's name on it – it was the one produced.
[Property produced and sworn to.]

PRISONER: I leave myself to the mercy of the Court.

GUILTY: DEATH, AGE 21. First Middlesex Jury, before Mr. Recorder.3

Since the clockmaking venture was a family business, it is necessary to mention John and Esther's other two sons, William and Robert, before continuing with the story of Isaac. Unlike Louis, they chose to live and work in Kent. Possibly they drew comfort from living as close as possible to the shores of the land of their ancestors. William was apprenticed to John Wontner of 127 Minories, City Wall, London in 1787 'for the consideration of one penny'.[4] Later he lived and worked in Dover, where he met and married Elizabeth Reynolds in the parish Church of St Mary. According to the parish records they had four children who all died before they were eighteen.

Robert followed in his brothers' footsteps. He was the twelve-year-old boy who tried to catch the thief who stole a watch from his father John's shop in Shadwell. He and his wife, Anne, and their six children lived at 164 Snargate Street in Dover, Kent. Robert is noted in the 1841 census at the age of sixty-five as still living at the same address with his daughter, Caroline, and sons Adolphus and Edwin who were also clockmakers. There is a quaint reference to Robert in a book entitled *Jorrocks' Jaunts and Jollities* by R. S. Surtees, which was first published in 1843 and reads:

As the coach approached Charlton Gate, the guard flourished his bugle and again struck up Rule Britannia which lasted the whole breadth of the marketplace, and length of Snargate Street, drawing from Mr. Muddle's shop the few loiterers who yet remained, and causing Mr. Le Plastrier, the patriotic moth impaler, to suspend the examination of the bowels of a watch, as they rattled past his window.[5]

Robert also became a famous entomologist and is mentioned in a letter dated 30 September 1831 from a Reverend W. R. Bree in a copy of the 1832 *Natural History Magazine*: 'Mr Curtis has named a moth *Salania Leplastriana* after Mr Le Plastrier of Snargate Street, who is very knowledgeable about moths.'[6]

Isaac was handsome, charming, and a bit of a dandy, with a definite entrepreneurial streak. *Finch and Holden's Directories* record him working in Deal in the early 1800s where he served his apprenticeship and learned his trade from his brothers William and Robert. The Le Plastriers built exquisite, intricate clocks and watches. Isaac was responsible for many of them, including a magnificent, mahogany, longcase grandfather clock purchased for 150 pounds by a Trinity House pilot, Richard Gilling, who lived in Deal. He also repaired a valuable clock belonging to lieutenant general Sir John Moore, and proudly delivered it to him before he departed for Spain and his death at the Battle of Corunna during the Peninsular War.

Isaac obviously had an adventurous side to his character, as at the age of seventeen he joined the East India Company as a midshipman, taking over a year to sail from Deal to Calcutta and back. The Company received a Royal Charter from Queen Elizabeth in 1600 and was the largest and most powerful shipping and trading organisation of its kind, sailing to India and China laden with household goods, and returning with spices, indigo, sugar, silk, ivory, and opium. Captains were the elite of the maritime world and were entitled to a thirteen-gun salute and a guard of honour on arrival at every port.

They were also given huge privileges – the most profitable of which was the shipping of fifty tons and returning with twenty tons for their own gain. They made the most of this generous bonus, especially when anchored in Deal waiting for the homeward-bound tide for London. The captains lavishly wined and dined the revenue boarding officer, while their contraband was clandestinely unloaded and smuggled into one of the tunnels which were connected to some of the respectable-looking houses. Isaac possibly learned his smooth and opportunistic ways from his time working for the East India Company.

Isaac and his eldest brother Louis were obsessed with the idea of reclaiming the three properties that were appropriated from Jean and Rachel after they fled France in 1685. Isaac's first wife, the arrestingly pretty Frances Trappit, was very much against the idea and tried to dissuade her husband from pursuing what some would say was a foolhardy plan. Frances was born in Deal and she and Isaac married in 1806 when both were twenty-one. She died five years later after giving Isaac three sons: William Louis, Charles Isaac, and John Christopher. I am descended from William Louis. Frances brought a dowry of sixteen thousand pounds – roughly one and a half million pounds today – to the marriage. No doubt Isaac hoped that she would allow him to use some, if not all, to raise funds for the court case. By making her children wards in chancery* she shrewdly made sure that all her assets would go directly to them when they reached twenty-one, and not be jeopardised by her husband's quest for justice. This was a very drastic step to take, and Isaac must have been mortified. He and his children left Kent for central London shortly after Frances died. Unfortunately, her predictions proved correct when in 1812 Isaac and Louis decided to travel to the courts of Rouen.

---

*   Wards in chancery – putting minors under the Court of Chancery, nowadays usually referred to as wards of court. Estates were administered under supervision of the Court.

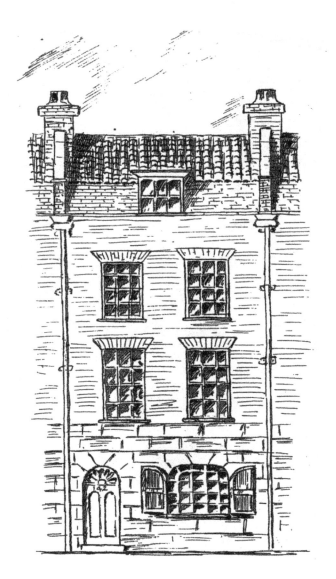

142 High Street, Shadwell, East London; the home of Louis Le Plastrier in 1802.

George III mahogany longcase clock, marked
Le Plastrier, London.
Recorded in Baillie's Watchmakers and
Clockmakers of the World, London, 1787.

A Regency mahogany bracket clock. 'It has a gilt metal pineapple finial and gadrooned
caddy top above a circular convex door enclosing a seven-inch white enamel dial.'[7] This
clock was made by my great-great-great-grandfather Isaac Le Plastrier, c.1807.

SNARGATE STREET, DOVER

The street where Robert Le Plastrier,
'the patriotic moth impaler,' lived and worked, c.1824.

Salania Leplastriana named after Robert Le Plastrier,
'the patriotic moth impaler,' c.1831.

Le Plastrier Watchpapers at the Minories and Mark Lane.

Isaac Le Plastrier with his second wife, Jane Agate.

CHAPTER THREE

The Court Case, And The Appeal

That tore asunder countless families arraying relatives against relatives, for the purpose of getting possession of their goods.[1]

H. M. Baird

It is said that every Le Plastrier, man and woman, was true to their Protestant faith, and that some died defending it. However, it is known that at least one – mentioned in chapter sixteen – renounced her faith and remained in France, and who can blame her. Marie Le Plastrier, daughter of Denys Le Plastrier and Elizabeth Conguard was married to Robert Du Garde. Both converted after the Revocation, and the authorities awarded them the properties that had once belonged to Jean and Rachel.

Isaac and Louis assumed they were the rightful heirs to these valuable residences, and it is understandable that they felt justified in attempting to retrieve what had been confiscated from their ancestors. It would not have been possible or judicious for them to have instigated legal proceedings any earlier, as France remained vehemently Catholic. This changed after Louis XVI and Marie Antoinette were sent to the guillotine in October 1793, and Napoleon Bonaparte came to power. Crucially, Napoleon was perceptive enough to appreciate the value of bringing Huguenots back to boost the declining economy. He advertised throughout Europe, encouraging them to reclaim assets seized after Louis XIV revoked the Edict of Nantes in 1685. As far as I know, very few bothered or had the finances to act on his proposal. I think Isaac and Louis were incredibly brave, although this has been a debatable point in the family ever since.

The defendant was Robert Jacques Du Garde, great-grandson of Robert and Marie Du Garde, whose extensive family had inherited the assets that once belonged to Jean. The plaintiff was recorded as Louis Le Plastrier, the elder of the two brothers. The properties they were trying to recover were:

1. Proche le Moulin, Jean and Rachel's country estate in the parish of Lacroix-Saint-Ouen, purchased by Jean from Isaac Papavoine in 1656.
2. Number 23 rue du Gros Horloge in the centre of Rouen. The house that is still standing, purchased by Jean from Pierre de la Mare in 1662.
3. A house at the corner of rue du Petit Salut and rue du Gros Horloge. This was supposedly the grandest and most desired of the three.

Louis and Isaac were confident that they would win the case and invested almost everything they owned in employing the best available barristers and advisors. Their legal team had to dig deep into the past to prepare the necessary documents, in order to establish that all three titles legally belonged to them. This seemed to be accepted without question by the judges, which is why it was such a shock to everyone present when the case was lost. One member of the council was so astonished at this unexpected outcome that he tore up his brief in disgust and stormed out of the court. Others argued that because the brothers were Protestants they were not entitled to ownership.

Colonel H. A. Du Pont surmises, in his book *The Early Generations of the Du Pont and Allied Families*, that the third house was possibly never owned by Jean, but by another senior relative. I think it is extremely unlikely that the barristers would have included it in the proceedings, and certainly not a second time in the appeal, if in any doubt that it was once owned by Jean and Rachel. Jean owned at least three residences, and it is very possible that he bought the third from his relative when he died.

I believe that they lost the case because too many years had elapsed since the properties had been ceded to Marie and Robert Du Garde, whose family had subsequently lived in and cared for them. Disastrously, Isaac and Louis decided to appeal the decision.

Meanwhile, in October 1813 in recognition of the outstanding success he had achieved with the manufacture of his beautiful timepieces, Isaac was admitted to the Freedom of the City of London and became a Freeman of the Worshipful Company of Clockmakers, which entailed many special privileges. Only freemen had jurisdiction over municipal affairs, including the right to elect mayors and members of parliament; the right to levy taxes; the administration of justice; and the right to conduct business within the city walls. Two years later he was noted as working for John Wontner at 127 Minories, where his brother William had been apprenticed.

Isaac married his second wife, the striking and accomplished Jane Agate, in 1816 at St George's Hanover Square. She was the daughter of Peter Agate of Stiddolph Heath, Sevenoaks, where the Agates had farmed for generations. Jane was evidently equally optimistic that her husband would win the appeal, as she allowed her dowry of twelve thousand pounds to be used to help pay for the spiralling costs of the second court case.

Undeterred at losing the first case, and on the advice of their legal team, Louis and Isaac appealed to the Court of Senior Jurisdiction in 1816. However, the timing was bad as their ally Napoleon had been deposed and exiled by the English to Saint Helena, after being defeated at Waterloo the previous year. Many influential friends were advising the brothers including Baron Du Fossé, who was related to the family by marriage. This would not have pleased the court, as aristocrats were not popular so soon after the Revolution. After spending eleven days in court, they lost the appeal.

This must have been an enormous disappointment to the family. In desperation the brothers held several meetings with their advisors, and as a last resort with the Foreign Secretary, Lord Castlereagh who, although sympathetic, was unable to help. They were so convinced of their rights that they even discussed the possibility of a second appeal.

In early October 1823 they crossed the English Channel on the *Lord Melville* to visit their old friend and advisor Baron Du Fossé. They travelled by diligence, which was a large enclosed coach pulled by four horses. It consisted of a coupé in the front seating three passengers, a middle coach seating six passengers, and a rotund behind seating a further six people. The driver rode on a seat directly above the front wheels and a conductor sat on a bench at the back with the baggage piled up behind him.

The brothers stayed at the Hôtel Robert in Boulogne for the first night. On the second night 'they stopped at an inn where they consumed tea, supper and breakfast, and later carried a fowl with bread for the journey to Dieppe,'[2] before proceeding to Rouen, where the baron lived. They stayed at the Hôtel de l'Europe where several meetings were held with Monsieur Le Carpenton, a barrister. On 6 October they dined with the baron before calling on Monsieur Le Carpenton for further talks. The following day the four men engaged in a conversation at the Hôtel Le Cheval Blanc in rue Beauvoisine over breakfast. It was at this meeting that the brothers were persuaded not to proceed with a second appeal. It may well be that the Du Garde family retain the titles to the Le Plastriers' assets to this day.

Most family papers and books written about the court case conclude that the vast amount of money spent on trying to retrieve the family estates eventually ruined Louis and Isaac financially. The family lore is that Isaac was a good-for-nothing opportunist, and a fortune-hunting wastrel who was kept by his second wife, Jane. I don't share those sentiments and cannot help admiring him for having had the courage to try and reclaim the properties, particularly as all their advisors were so positive. Having done much research on the subject, I believe that Isaac was an entrepreneur at heart, sometimes a foolhardy one, who strove for success which constantly eluded him. He certainly was not idle as he made timepieces almost until the day he died. Although the family lived in the most expensive parts of London and sent their many children to the best schools and colleges, Isaac died almost destitute many years later, as did his brother Louis.

Louis's eldest son Louis continued working with his father in Shadwell until he emigrated to Melbourne on the first non-convict ship with his wife and six children in 1848. Subsequent to the departure of his son and grandchildren, Louis senior is noted at the age of seventy as being a 'Poor Brother' living at The Charterhouse in Holborn. He died at the age of eighty-four and is buried in the grounds of the chapel. Charterhouse is a magnificent fourteenth-century building which, when Louis resided there, was a home for eighty male pensioners; 'gentlemen by descent and in poverty, soldiers who have borne arms by sea or land, merchants decayed by piracy or shipwreck, or servants in household to the king or queens' majesty, and to educate forty boys.'[3] I am not sure how Louis was fortunate enough to end his life there, but it is comforting to know that he was. This was the beginning of the famous school Charterhouse in Godalming, Surrey. The original building is now home to forty male pensioners, known as 'Brothers'.

CHAPTER FOUR

⬦━◉━⬦━◇━━━◇━◉━⬦

The Downward Spiral

The strange and unforeseen vicissitudes that befell the Huguenots in the latter part of the seventeenth century placed them in a situation presenting certain marked points of resemblance to the condition of their fathers in the early part of the eighteenth century.[1]

H. M. Baird

During the disastrous appeal, Isaac and Jane lived in the parish of St Botolph without Aldgate. Isaac continued working for Wontner's until 1819 when the family moved to 63 Mark Lane, St Olave, close to the small medieval Protestant church in Hart Street. The area was where the Worshipful Company of Clockmakers was located, and where a tight-knit community of wealthy Huguenots lived. Samuel Pepys, the famous diarist, had lived in Seething Street, St Olave, in 1660. Isaac started his own business while living at Mark Lane. As the Le Plastriers were renowned for their superior timepieces, he had no problem establishing a business.

St Olave was an expensive area, and among other staff Isaac employed a footman, David Plummer, at ten guineas a year – a privilege usually reserved for the very rich. He was obviously living beyond his means and could not afford such an indulgence, as he was forced to dispense with Plummer's services, owing him ten months' pay. Since Isaac was unable to raise the money to pay the footman, he was deemed penniless and spent many months in a grim and filthy workhouse in Hoxton. Beds were swamped with vermin and inmates ate with their fingers, as no knives and forks were provided for the meagre meals that were served. Having been used to the niceties of life this must have been extremely degrading and upsetting for him. On 21 January 1829 Isaac received his settlement papers. His debt had been paid, possibly with the help of Huguenot friends.

Jane and Isaac had five children: Francis, George, Thomas, Jane, and Frances. All the children apart from Frances were born in St Olave. She was born just after Isaac experienced financial problems with his footman, when the family moved to Blackfriars, not far from St Olave.

It was clear that Isaac could not be relied on to provide for his family in the manner to which they were accustomed. Although it was not considered genteel for cultured wives to work, Jane came to the rescue and started using her considerable talent as a seamstress. She soon established a successful couturier and milliner business, designing and making clothes for aristocratic ladies. The family's fortunes vastly improved and in 1832 they moved to 20 Ludgate Hill, close to St Paul's Cathedral, where Jane ran her business and Isaac continued making clocks and watches. They also purchased a property in the country. It seems that history was repeating itself, as in 1833 Thomas Jones, aged twenty-five, was sentenced to death at the Old Bailey for stealing from Isaac's shop:

Thomas Jones was indicted for feloniously breaking and entering the
dwelling-house of Isaac Le Plastrier, on the 11th of April 1833, at

St Martin, Ludgate, and stealing therein 2 watch cases, value 4 l the goods of the said Isaac Le Plastrier and another.

ROBERT CURRY: *I live at No. 45 Dean Street, Soho, and am a turner. On the 11th of April, about four o'clock in the afternoon, I was going down Ludgate Hill, and saw the prisoner force his hands through the window of Mr Le Plastrier's shop – I could not perceive what he took out, but I saw that he had got something; I took him into the shop – the shop door was not shut at the time; I saw him endeavour to conceal what he had got, and I found a watchcase in each of his hands. I marked them and delivered them to the constable; he forced his hands through a very large square of glass which he broke.*

MR ISAAC LE PLASTRIER: *I am a watchmaker and live at No. 20 Ludgate Hill. When I returned from the country this morning after this happened, I found that one of the panes of glass in my shop window was broken into one hundred and fifty pieces. My son, who lives in the house, and I carry on the business in partnership. The lease of it is mine, but the rent and taxes are paid out of the business.*

JAMES SNOW: *I am a constable and live in Holyday Yard. I received the prisoner in charge and produce the watch cases which I received from Curry.*

MR ISAAC LE PLASTRIER: *These are my cases – they are worth 4 l; the door which opens onto the street does not at once admit you into the shop – there is a lobby, and on the right there is a door which enters the shop; the outer door is always open – the house is in the parish of St Martin, Ludgate.*

ROBERT CURRY, re-examined: *Which door do you mean was open? I meant the outer door — the inner door was closed, and the window was closed, but the street door was open.*

PRISONER: I did it through distress – I had been out of work for a long time and did not know what to do to get a bit of bread.

GUILTY: DEATH. Aged 25. First Middlesex Jury, before Mr. Recorder2

The son referred to above is my great-great-grandfather William Louis, who worked with his father. Their wares seem to have been very popular with thieves. I also read that in 1824 Daniel Morgan and James Sessions were both found guilty of stealing a watch worth one pound from Isaac and were transported to Australia for seven years. On 15 April 1830, Robert Wall was found guilty of receiving goods worth forty pounds including one skeleton clock, five other clocks, four timepieces, one barometer, one watch, and two sacks. Robert Wall was transported to Australia for fourteen years. I don't know if the thief was ever caught, but if he was, he would have been sentenced to death like Thomas Jones.

Isaac inevitably suffered from the theft of so many of his clocks and watches, as it is recorded that he spent time in Fleet Prison having again been late in paying his debts. With permission, it was sometimes possible for prisoners to continue running their business while confined, thereby earning enough money to pay for their incarceration in addition to the accrued debt. This may have been what Isaac did, or possibly Jane or his Huguenot friends bailed him out – we will never know. He was discharged on 14 January 1836.

Isaac continued making and selling his timepieces, while Jane became increasingly successful as a milliner and dressmaker. In need of assistance, she enlisted the help of some of her children. When George was on holiday from Churchfields Academy, he made cap springs to keep his mother's millinery creations in good shape. Frances and Jane designed and stitched hats and gowns, and the latter eventually started her own successful business at 98 New Bond Street. Their brother Francis became an accomplished carpenter, making furniture from 20 Ludgate Hill until he married and later joined his cousin Louis, the younger, and his family in Melbourne.

In 1841 Isaac and his family moved to 21 Holles Street, Cavendish Square, where Jane became dressmaker and embroiderer to Queen Adelaide, wife of William IV. She later made garments and hats for Queen Victoria, and was recorded as 'Madame Jane Le Plastrier, Milliner, Dress, and Corset Maker to Her Majesty'[3]. Jane employed staff and worked from impressive properties she rented, namely, 12 Park Terrace in Regent's Park and 33 Rathbone Place. She was expected to provide luxurious fitting rooms in discreet and expensive areas where royal and aristocratic clients could discuss their requirements in privacy, but she visited Queen Adelaide and Queen Victoria at Windsor Castle or Buckingham Palace, where they had more privacy.

Ten years later everything changed, and Isaac and Jane were living at 37 Arlington Street, Camden, with their daughters Jane and Frances, aged twenty-five and twenty-two respectively. Jane was fifty-eight and Isaac seventy-two. Isaac was still working, but Jane had retired. I can't help wondering if Isaac's misfortunes eventually affected Jane's successful business. They both died, aged eighty, Isaac in 1857 and Jane in 1872. They are buried with their daughter Jane, who died unmarried at the age of forty-two, in the Metropolitan Cemetery, West Norwood, Lambeth, where many Le Plastriers are interred. It is now one of the Magnificent Seven Cemeteries of London, and of great architectural and ecological interest.

The clockmaking business waxed and waned over the years and Isaac, like his brother Louis, seems to have died leaving nothing but a few personal effects.

CHAPTER FIVE

William Louis Le Plastrier
And His Brothers

*The greater part of the manufacturing establishments have
been transported by the Protestant refugees to foreign lands.*[1]

H. M. Baird

Illiam Louis, Charles Isaac, and John Christopher from
Isaac's first marriage to Frances Trappit, continued to
live with their father, their stepmother Jane, and their
half-siblings. The three brothers inherited their mother's fortune on
their twenty-first birthdays, as she had wisely guaranteed that her
husband would not receive a penny. However, they all squandered or
lost it in one way or another.

Charles Isaac married Harriet Grimshaw, whose father was a
naval surgeon working under Nelson during the Battle of Trafalgar.
Shortly before they married Charles lost most of his inheritance when
he unsuccessfully attempted to introduce horse-drawn omnibuses in
London. The venture failed, leaving him in debt, after he had entrusted

his plans to a dishonest coachbuilder who brought his omnibuses out before Charles. Disillusioned, he and Harriet decided to emigrate to Tobago where several of Harriet's relatives lived.

Charles applied and was accepted for the job as Deputy Provost Marshal of Tobago, and the family left England in April 1832. After a long and dangerous journey, they arrived in mid-September in spectacular fashion after their ship hit a large rock and sank. Fortunately, they were rescued but lost everything they owned. Despite such a dramatic start Charles prospered, and eventually became the Honourable Charles Isaac Le Plastrier. To his pride and delight he was later given the honour of reading the Proclamation of The Freedom of Slaves. Charles and Harriet produced four children and lived happily in Tobago until they died. One of their daughters, Harriet, known as Poppy, was particularly vivacious and attractive, yet never married. She died in England, at the age of ninety. It is noted that my grandfather George Ernest Ramsay, who lived in Kenya, and another relative paid for her burial and memorial in the Metropolitan Cemetery.

Charles's half-brother George – the son who helped his mother, Jane, with the cap springs for her hats – also emigrated to Tobago where he married a Creole woman. At the time this was not accepted in social circles and he would not have been invited to any of his brother's smart diplomatic events, where royalty were occasionally guests. George died in 1885 in Nimba, Liberia.

John Christopher is reputed to have been a brilliant engineer who predicted that within a few years England would be dissected in all directions by railways. At the time of his death in 1830 there was only one railway with a single steam engine, running a distance of approximately ten miles from Stockton to Darlington, so his foresight was amazing. He died, aged twenty-one, unmarried and childless.

William Louis was the only one of the three brothers to continue making timepieces. On completing his apprenticeship, which commenced when he was fifteen, he worked with Isaac at Ludgate Hill before joining AB Savory & Sons in Cornhill, where he remained

Sophia Le Plastrier, née Merry, my great-great-grandmother,
wife of William Louis, c. 1890.

My great-grandmother Clara Jeronomy Le Plastrier, c. 1880.

Clara Jeronomy and George Ramsay with their children, from right back row, Edith Alice, my grandfather's twin, Clara Jeronomy, Arthur, Clara Eleanor, Elizabeth Sophie, and Winifred May. Bottom row from left, Gertrude Grace, George, and Beatrice. My grandfather George Ernest took the photo in 1898 before leaving for Kenya to work as an accountant for The Uganda Railway, aged twenty-two.

until 1843. He then started his own business. While living with his father, Isaac recklessly persuaded him to invest the large amount he inherited when he was twenty-one in a risky jewellery venture, which failed. It was unfortunate that Frances was no longer alive to advise her son. She would certainly have warned him against entering into any business arrangement with his irresponsible father.

William carried on the family name in style by marrying Sophia Merry in 1836 at St Ann Blackfriars. They produced ten children including my great-grandmother Clara Jeronomy. Tragically, they lost two of their children in childhood; Anna Maria, aged seven, in January 1856 and five-year-old Mary Harriet, three days later. The family lived at 22 Chancery Lane, between Westminster and Camden, where they remained until William's death at the age of forty-nine. He left very little, which is not surprising as it must have been extremely expensive to feed and educate so many children. Rather poignantly, he wrote that he desired to be buried plainly but with decency. As requested, he was interred with dignity amongst many Le Plastriers, in the Metropolitan Cemetery.

William's eighteen-year-old son Charles continued with his father's business while living with his mother, Sophia, in Islington until his untimely death in 1864 at the age of twenty-six. Sophia must have been heartbroken at losing him when so young and having already lost her husband and two small daughters. Towards the end of her life, she lived with her daughter Clara Jeronomy and her husband, George Ramsay, my great-grandparents. Clara was the last person in my immediate family to have held the Le Plastrier surname.

PART THREE

Australia 1848

CHAPTER ONE

Le Plastriers In Melbourne

The countries whither they went were enriched by the arts
and trades which the French refugees introduced.[1]

H. M. Baird

T here are presently more Le Plastrier descendants in Australia than anywhere else in the world due to Louis, son of Louis of court case fame, emigrating with his wife Georgina Woods and their six children aged between twelve and twenty-three.

It remains a mystery why Louis made the decision to leave his elderly father, brother, and sisters, as well as the country that had given his family sanctuary. It was a drastic and courageous step to contemplate starting a new life in an unknown and undeveloped country at the other end of the world, especially with such a large family. Social unrest existed all over Europe, and there was an outbreak of cholera at the time that claimed 52,000 lives in England and Wales, which could have been why they left. I cannot help comparing this awful outbreak, and the plague, mentioned earlier, with the worldwide Covid-19 pandemic that we are experiencing as I write.

On 8 November 1848 the family boarded the clipper, the *Lord Hungerford*, and sailed from Plymouth to Melbourne. She weighed 707 tons and was over 320 feet long with a beam measuring fifty feet. I can imagine Louis, Georgina, and their children clinging tearfully to the rest of the family at the dock. Sailors carried aboard crates of noisy hens, pigs, sheep, and cattle to be consumed and milked during the long voyage, while the passengers' precious luggage was loaded on board. The great sails flapped farewell as the ship sailed into the unknown, the family waving desperately to the diminishing figures of their loved ones on the dock. They all knew that they were unlikely to meet again.

After a long and arduous voyage, the clipper docked on 10 February 1849 at Hobsons Bay, on the edge of a small settlement of pioneers living in shabby tents – Melbourne!

The *Lord Hungerford* was the first ship to convey paying passengers. After her arrival, *The Melbourne Daily News* reported: 'The parties who came out of her are of an extremely reasonable class and are the first to arrive under the co-operation system.'[2] The passengers were so delighted by the wonderful attention they had received from Captain Patterson during the voyage that 'they intended to present him with a "piece of plate" to show their appreciation.'[3]

Louis and Georgina found it extremely hard starting life in a strange country with so many children, and very little money, but they were blessed with the fortitude of their Huguenot ancestors which gave them the strength to survive and prosper. They bought some grazing land, pitched a couple of tents, and began to farm cattle. Many years later one of their sons, another Louis, reminisced to his son Arthur that as a child he used to 'drive bullocks with mud up to their middles'[4] through what is now one of the main streets, Collins Street. Many of Louis and Georgina's descendants preferred commerce to farming, which is not surprising with hundreds of years of it steeped in their blood, and some eventually became some leading merchants in the city

The second family to follow their cousins was Francis, the carpenter – Isaac and Jane's eldest son – his pregnant wife, Eliza Hill, and their daughters four-year-old Marion and Eliza Jane, aged one. The family sailed on the tiny barque, the *Emma Goodwin*, on 13 April 1853. Maybe they were also escaping cholera which was again rampant in London. Francis's sister Jane, his mother and my great-great-grandfather William arrived at the East India docks to wish them *bon voyage*. The *Emma Goodwin* had dropped anchor down river to Gravesend to await favourable winds, so there was a considerable delay in setting sail. After a long wait, Francis and his young family eventually boarded the barque and joined the excited voices of their fellow passengers. With the smell of the salty sea all around them, they sailed away to the wailing and screeching of the seagulls, their family waving frantically from the docks until the barque was out of sight.

After a lengthy and dangerous journey, the family arrived at Port Phillip on 11 September. Eliza, who had been four months pregnant when they left, presented Francis with a daughter Ellen the day before they docked. Sadly, the child died before her second birthday. They were not as fortunate as their cousins because to begin with Francis could not find any work. They started their life in a tent on the beach and became so impoverished that the local baker kindly kept them alive by giving them bread. They existed on this, and by catching fish and selling them in the village. Francis went on to make a good living through his carpentry and cabinet making skills. He lived until he was ninety-nine, and died at his house, Tivoli, in Green Street, Ivanhoe. In one of his letters, he reminisced that when they first arrived, 'there was not a crust of bread nor even a sixpence in the house.'[5] Edward and his brother Frank, sons of William and Sophia, also later emigrated to Australia.

What courage my kinsmen must have possessed to flee the country of their birth in such challenging circumstances, and then much later to leave the safety of England in small sailing ships to face an uncertain future.

Like all families, the Le Plastriers had their ups and downs, both personally and financially, as will future generations, but the blood of our brave ancestors will always run in their veins.

EPILOGUE

Clara Jeronomy Le Plastrier, known as Auntie Jonty, married George Ramsay, on 28 September 1872 in London. He was a wealthy wine merchant and Freeman of the City of London.

Their eight children, including my grandfather George Ernest and his twin Edith Alice, were all born in Chelsea.

George Ernest was training as an accountant in central London, when he met my grandmother Alice Muriel Norman. They were soon engaged, and to the delight of both families began planning their wedding. However, everything changed when George happened to see an advertisement in *The Times*, inserted by the British Government, looking for people to work in the newly opened East African Protectorate. Although he knew nothing about that part of the world, having always had a thirst for adventure he was quick to respond to this opportunity.

It was not long before he was offered a position by the Foreign Office to work as an accountant for the Uganda Railway, based in an area which was later named Nairobi. His new job was to curtail the spiralling costs of building the new railway line which had been started in Mombasa in 1896. The line was due to arrive in Nairobi in 1900 before continuing on to Uganda.

The courage and valour of his Le Plastrier ancestors was in George's blood, and to the surprise of his family and his fiancée he had no hesitation in accepting the job. Although heartbroken, Alice promised to join him as soon as it was considered safe – this was four years later.

In 1899 at the age of twenty-two George left the comfort of his home in London with nothing but a tent, a gun, and very little money to start his new life in what was then known as 'darkest Africa'. He was one of the first white people to arrive in Nairobi which was then a barren, dangerous place, teeming with poisonous snakes, scorpions, and millions of wild animals, including man-eating lions. The only human inhabitants were threatening, near-naked, suspicious African tribes, who had never seen a white face, and carried poisonous arrows.

His contract was initially for five years, but no one, least of all my grandfather, imagined that he would fall under the thrall of Africa and remain there until the end of his life. Alice joined him in June 1804, and they married at the Mombasa Cathedral soon after her arrival. George Norman was born in May 1905 and my father, Derek, in September 1912. The story of our family life in Kenya over the following four generations is continued in the *Forgotten Pioneer*.

SOURCE NOTES

Cover

'*A Huguenot, on St Bartholomew's Day*': Rosenfeld, *John Everett Millais*, 68.

Introduction

1 'do as they wished': Le Plastrier Webb, *The Le Plastrier and Allied Families*, 8.

Prologue: Delving Into The Past

PART ONE FRANCE 1395–1685

Origins Of The Le Plastrier Family

1 'The Huguenots were': Baird, *The Huguenots and the Revocation of the Edict of Nantes*, [vol 2] 3.
2 'Lorens Hèrouf': Le Plastrier Webb, *The Le Plastrier and Allied Families*, 1.

The Siege Of Rouen

1 'France was': Baird, *The Huguenots and the Revocation of the Edict of Nantes,* [vol 2] 3.
2 'It is you we want': Catherine Bearne, *Pictures of the Old French Court,* 238.

Jehan Le Plastrier, The Entrepreneur

1 'Scarcely could': Baird, *The Huguenots and the Revocation of the Edict of Nantes,* [vol 2] 3.
2 'The voice told me': Pernoud, *Joan of Arc: By Herself and Her Witnesses,* 30.
3 'Joan the Maid came to Vaucouleurs': ibid., 33–34.
4 'To introduce a prophetess to the impressionable Charles': Vale, *Charles VII,* 50.
5 'Robert twice refused': Pernoud, *Joan of Arc: By Herself and Her Witnesses,* 34.
6 'Robert de Baudricourt caused those': ibid., 39.
7 'I was myself present': Pernoud and Clin, *Joan of Arc: Her Story,* 22.
8 'Alas! Do they treat me': Pernoud, *Joan of Arc: By Herself and Her Witnesses,* 228.
9 'Bishop, I die by you': ibid.

Onset Of The Persecution Of The Huguenots

1 'Personal and Family': Baird, *The Huguenots and the Revocation of Nantes* [vol 2] 275.
2 'It is said': Le Plastrier Webb, *The Le Plastrier and Allied Families,* 75.
3 'Some of them': ibid., 65.
4 'the greatest match': Roeder, *Catherine de' Medici and the Lost Revolution,* 35.
5 'worth a kingdom': Van Dyke, *Catherine de Médicis,* [vol 1] 23.
6 'late that night': Roeder, *Catherine de' Medici and the Lost Revolution,* 38.

7   'These people': Whitehead, *Gaspard de Coligny, Admiral of France*, 130.

8   '*J'ai reçu la fille toute nue*': Roeder, *Catherine de' Medici and the Lost Revolution*, 41.

9   'She was very good on horseback': Bourdeïlle and Saint-Beuve, *Illustrious Dames of the Court of the Valois Kings*, 53.

10 'tradesmen who are not fit to call themselves': Héritier, *Catherine de' Medici*, 67.

11 'women rather than years': Van Dyke, *Catherine de Médicis*, [vol 1] 47.

12 'In Protestant eyes': ibid., [vol 1] 68.

13 'Madame, rest satisfied': Williams, *Henry II: His Court and Times*, 234.

14 'vermin!': Van Dyke, *Catherine de Médicis*, [vol 1] 375.

'The Daughter Of Merchants'

1   'But when a ruler': Niccolò Machiavelli, *The Prince*, 11.

2   'dreamed that she saw him': Du Hausset, *Memoirs of Marguerite de Valois*, Letter V11.

3   'my friend': Bourdeïlle and Saint-Beuve, *Illustrious Dames of the Court of the Valois Kings*, 4.

4   'For the Guises': Whitehead, *Gaspard de Coligny, Admiral of France*, 73.

5   'the house of Guise ruleth': Knecht, *Catherine de' Medici*, 61.

6   'He is not well beloved': Whitehead, *Gaspard de Coligny, Admiral of France*, 33.

7   'This being the good pleasure': Sichel, *Catherine de' Medici and the French Reformation*, 101.

8   'Florentine shopkeeper': Héritier, *Catherine de' Medici*, 209.

9   '*Cette fille de marchands*': Roeder, *Catherine de' Medici and the Lost Revolution*, 81.

10 'So vulgar': ibid.

11 'Now is the time': Héritier, *Catherine de' Medici*, 111.

12 'revelled in a very orgy': Whitehead, *Gaspard de Coligny, Admiral of France*, 82.

13 'Oh God Most': Van Dyke, *Catherine de Médicis*, [vol 1] 154.

14 'I am astonished': ibid.
15 'They have slaughtered': Whitehead, *Gaspard de Coligny, Admiral of France*, 82.
16 'Ten, twenty': ibid.
17 'So extreme is the hatred': ibid., 84.
18 'Her son became': Du Hausset, *Memoirs of Marguerite de Valois*, Letter, 111.
19 'So far Huguenots': Whitehead, *Gaspard de Coligny, Admiral of France*, 88.
20 'When the Admiral': ibid.
21 'The assembly': ibid., 89.
22 'is the most cowardly': Roelker, *Queen of Navarre: Jeanne d'Albret*, 148.
23 'I have [come] this morning': Sichel, *Catherine de' Medici and the French Reformation*, 113.

'The Black Queen'

1 'Since a ruler has to be able': Niccolò Machiavelli, *The Prince*, 94.
2 'I want to tell you plainly': Van Dyke, *Catherine de Médicis*, [vol 1] 200 – 201.
3 'Too heavy': ibid., 210.
4 'In twenty cities': ibid., 203.
5 'I adjure you': Baird, *History of the Rise of the Huguenots*, [vol 1] 278.
6 'We say that His body': ibid., 286.
7 'I do not': Bourdeïlle and Saint-Beuve, *Illustrious Dames of the Court of the Valois Kings*, 80.
8 'In the eyes of the great and powerful': Héritier, *Catherine de' Medici*, 209.
9 'for her children, for France': ibid., 210.
10 '*Mon Père*': Roeder, *Catherine de' Medici and the Lost Revolution*, 429.
11 'the Cardinal de Châtillon': Whitehead, *Gaspard de Coligny, Admiral of France*, 93.
12 'There is one among the chiefs': ibid.
13 'They speak of God': ibid., 98.

14 'the whole Court was infected': Du Hausset, *Memoirs of Marguerite de Valois*, Letter 1.

15 'You will be carried off at midnight': Roeder, *Catherine de' Medici and the Lost Revolution*, 296.

16 'clearly understand': Van Dyke, *Catherine de Médicis*, [vol 1] 311.

The Beginning Of The End

1 'So if a leader': Niccolò Machiavelli, *The Prince*, 96.

2 'Kill! Kill!': Carroll, *Martyrs and Murderers: The Guise Family and the Making of Europe*, 18.

3 'it made Guise': Van Dyke, *Catherine de Médicis*, [vol 1] 240.

4 'But it was not only': ibid., 114.

5 'Where the Huguenot is Master': ibid., 117.

6 'The more turbulent': ibid., 104.

7 'He confessed that': ibid., 111.

8 'It was with good and sincere intentions': Héritier, *Catherine de' Medici*, 214.

9 'To begin with': ibid., 215.

10 'that if one drop of blood': Whitehead, *Gaspard de Coligny, Admiral of France*, 80.

11 'Antoine's connection': Héritier, *Catherine de' Medici*, 89.

12 'the whole city': Van Dyke, *Catherine de Médicis*, [vol 1] 242-243.

13 'the best man': ibid.

14 'save the children': ibid.

15 'burn this instantly': ibid., 242.

16 'It would be impossible to tell you': Whitehead, *Gaspard de Coligny, Admiral of France*, 117.

17 'he is falsely accused': Roelker, *Queen of Navarre: Jeanne d'Albret*, 207.

18 'This death is': Héritier, *Catherine de' Medici*, 221.

19 'she admitted': ibid., 223.

20 'if Monsieur de Guise': ibid.

21 'the craftiness': ibid., 208.

The Grand Royal Tour

1 'Actually, being feared': Niccolò Machiavelli, *The Prince*, 89.
2 'shepherdesses dressed in cloth of gold and satin': Du Hausset, *Memoirs of Marguerite de Valois*, Letter 1.

Escalation Of Oppression

1 'The contender': Niccolò Machiavelli, *The Prince*, 119.
2 'The Huguenots say': Whitehead, *Gaspard de Coligny, Admiral of France*, 230.
3 'the reason why': Van Dyke, *Catherine de Médicis*, [vol 1] 380.
4 'source, root, and origin': Whitehead, *Gaspard de Coligny, Admiral of France*, 198.
5 'It must be confessed that if you have': ibid., 197.
6 'bloody peace': ibid., 196.
7 'Her scheme was': ibid., 197.
8 'The stag is in the net': Van Dyke, *Catherine de Médicis*, [vol 1] 387.
9 'with a joy and ardour incredible': Whitehead, *Gaspard de Coligny, Admiral of France*, 198.
10 'Young as I am': Héritier, *Catherine de' Medici*, 268.
11 'For Christ and country!': Whitehead, *Gaspard de Coligny, Admiral of France*, 206.
12 'In both camps': Héritier, *Catherine de' Medici*, 283.
13 'It was the fiercest': Whitehead, *Gaspard de Coligny, Admiral of France*, 207.
14 'God will not leave unpunished': ibid., 197.
15 'It stated that': ibid., 228.

The Marriage Conspiracy

1 'Hence, if a': Niccolò Machiavelli, *The Prince*, 81.
2 'the King, my son': Roelker, *Queen of Navarre: Jeanne d'Albret*, 346.

3 'there is one thing': Roeder, *Catherine de' Medici and the Lost Revolution*, 429.

4 'You hide yourself': Sichel, *The Later Years of Catherine de' Medici*, 139.

5 'Better to die by a bold stroke': Whitehead, *Gaspard de Coligny, Admiral of France*, 237.

6 'is to be found each day': ibid., 238.

7 'I cannot imagine why': Roelker, *Queen of Navarre: Jeanne d'Albret*, 355.

8 'as for the beauty': ibid., 376.

9 'Not for anything': ibid., 373.

10 'they scratch me': ibid., 376.

11 'I am in agony': ibid., 372.

12 'I beg you': ibid., 381.

13 'we are very distressed': ibid.,392.

14 'her pure white face': Bourdeïlle and Saint-Beuve, *Illustrious Dames of the Court of the Valois Kings*, 161.

15 'the most unhappy woman': Chamberlin, *Marguerite of Navarre*, 270 – 71.

16 'Never did I consent': ibid.

St Bartholomew's Day Massacre

1 'A ruler mustn't': Niccolò Machiavelli, *The Prince*, 87.

2 'In Paris there are': Carroll, *Martyrs and Murderers: The Guise Family and the Making of Europe*, 200.

3 'I was set out': Du Hausset, *Memoirs of Marguerite de Valois*, Letter V.

4 'Accordingly, the Marshal': ibid.

5 'The Queen my mother': ibid.

6 'Kill the lot!': Héritier, *Catherine de' Medici*, 323.

7 'The Huguenots': Du Hausset, *Memoirs of Marguerite de Valois*, Letter V.

8 'whereupon they were': Whitehead, *Gaspard de Coligny, Admiral of France*, 268.

9 'a dozen leading': ibid.

10 'Men and women': ibid., 267.

11 'Everywhere': ibid., 268.

12 'It was enough to cry': ibid., 267.

13 'Five or six days afterwards': Du Hausset, *Memoirs of Marguerite de Valois*, Letter V.

Henri III, The Last Valois King

1 'Since a ruler': Niccolò Machiavelli, *The Prince*, 83.

2 'crimped and re-crimped': Van Dyke, *Catherine de Médicis*, [vol 2] 232.

3 'appeared after': ibid.

4 'With completely cold detachment': Héritier, *Catherine de' Medici*, 356.

5 'This occasioned': Du Hausset, *Memoirs of Marguerite de Valois*, Letter IX.

6 'The situation': Van Dyke, *Catherine de Médicis*, [vol 2] 189.

7 'The court': ibid.

8 'Accordingly, as soon as it was dusk': Du Hausset, *Memoirs of Marguerite de Valois*, Letter X.

9 'He is gone to make war': ibid.

10 'The King received him': ibid.

11 'Long live Guise': Carroll, *Martyrs and Murderers: The Guise Family and the Making of Europe*, 274.

12 'Good morning, Madame': Héritier, *Catherine de' Medici*,456.

13 'My son': ibid.

14 'no sooner': ibid., 468.

15 'I ask you': Bourdeïlle and Saint-Beuve, *Illustrious Dames of the Court of the Valois Kings*, 88.

16 'the Sorbonne proclaimed': Le Plastrier Webb, *The Le Plastrier and Allied Families*, 4.

'Paris Is Well Worth A Mass'

1 'In a day': Baird, *History of the Rise of the Huguenots*, [vol 1] 199.

2 '*Paris vaut bien une Messe*': Le Plastrier Webb, *The Le Plastrier and Allied Families*, 82.

3 'food, bed': ibid., 23.

4 'Pray God': ibid., 21.

5 'This Year of Grace': ibid., 29.

6 'Friday, 10th January 1613': ibid., 73–74.

7 'For those who may wish': ibid., 82.

Hopes Dashed

1 'Blood Flowed': Baird, *History of the Rise of the Huguenots*, [vol 1] 151.

2 'They did not': Pardoe, *Louis the Fourteenth, and the Court of France in the Seventeenth Century*, 49–50.

The Revocation Of The Edict Of Nantes

1 'A juncture had been reached': Baird, *The Huguenots and the Revocation of the Edict of Nantes*, [vol 2] 3.

2 'dropped his mask': ibid.

3 'Our subjects': Le Plastrier Webb, *The Le Plastrier and Allied Families*, 77.

4 'Fine words': ibid.

5 'His majesty has been annoyed': Baird, *The Huguenots and the Revocation of the Edict of Nantes*, 5.

6 'If this does not induce you': ibid.

7 'The scandals': ibid., 16.

8 'Ah Madame': ibid.

9 'In as much': ibid., 27.

10 'Such was the edict of recall': ibid., 30.

11 'the undersigned': ibid., 46.

12 'The mask was dropped': ibid., 45.

13 'Persecution was not now': ibid., 32.

14 'You are not': ibid., 6.

15 'I have this morning condemned': ibid., 56.

16 'The Protestant could stay': Carolyn Chappell Lougee, *Facing the Revocation, Huguenot Families, Faith, and the King's Will*, 41.

Braving Escape

1 'Soldiers of the king': Baird, *The Huguenots and the Revocation of the Edict of Nantes*, [vol 2] 4.

2 '*Le Roi le veut!*': ibid., 45.

3 'The King's wish': Le Plastrier Webb, *The Le Plastrier and Allied Families*, 79.

4 'I confess to my shame': Baird, *The Huguenots and the Revocation of the Edict of Nantes*, [vol 2] 44.

5 'Known to all Rouen': Le Plastrier Webb, *The Le Plastriers and Allied Families*, 81.

6 'Suffice to say': Baird, *The Huguenots and the Revocation of the Edict of Nantes*, [vol 2] 73.

7 'Delicate women': ibid., 74.

8 'It was no rare thing': ibid., 72.

9 'Many of the sufferers': ibid., 47.

PART TWO ENGLAND 1685–1872

Freedom

1 'It has been well said': Baird, *The Huguenots and the Revocation of the Edict of Nantes*, [vol 2] 105.

2 'Robert Le Plastrier': Le Plastrier Webb, *The Le Plastrier and Allied Families*, 92.

The Clockmakers

1 'Foreign trade': Baird, *The Huguenots and the Revocation of the Edict of Nantes*, [vol 2] 100.
2 'Benjamin Baker': Courtesy Wikipedia [in the public domain].
3 'William Smith': ibid.
4 'for the consideration': Le Plastrier Webb, *The Le Plastrier and Allied Families*, 93.
5 'As the coach': R.S. Surtees, *Jorrocks's Jaunts and Jollities*, 111.
6 'Mr Curtis': Le Plastrier Webb, *The Le Plastrier and Allied Families*, 93.

The Court Case, And The Appeal

1 'That tore asunder': Baird, *The Huguenots and the Revocation of the Edict of Nantes*, [vol 2] 106.
2 'they stopped': Le Plastrier Webb, *The Le Plastrier and Allied Families*, 98.
3 'gentlemen by descent': Courtesy of Wikipedia [in the public domain].

The Downward Spiral

1 'The strange and unforseen vicissitudes': Baird, *The Huguenots and the Revocation of the Edict of Nantes*, [vol 2] 155.
2 'Thomas Jones': Courtesy Wikipedia [in the public domain].
3 'Madame Jane': Le Plastrier Webb, *The Le Plastrier and Allied Families*, 96.

William Louis Le Plastrier And His Brothers

1 'The greater part': Baird, *The Huguenots and the Revocation of the Edict of Nantes*, [vol 2] 77.

PART THREE AUSTRALIA 1848

Le Plastriers In Melbourne

1 'The countries whither they went': Baird, *The Huguenots and the Revocation of the Edict of Nantes*, [vol 2] 101.
2 'The parties who came': Le Plastrier Webb, *The Le Plastrier and Allied Families*, 138.
3 'they intended to present him': ibid.
4 'drive bullocks': ibid.
5 'there was not a crust': ibid., 145.

SELECTED BIBLIOGRAPHY

Baird, Henry, M, *History of the Rise of the Huguenots*, [vol 1], A Mystical World Reprints, 2017
—— *The Huguenots and the Revocation of the Edict of Nantes*, Vol. 11, Charles Scribner's Sons, New York, 1895.

Bearne, Catherine, *Pictures of the Old French Court: Jeanne de Bourbon, Isabeau de Bavière, Anne de Bretagne*, T. Fisher Unwin, London, 1900.

Bourdeïlle, Pierre de, and C.A. Sainte-Beuve, *Illustrious Dames of the Court of the Valois Kings*. Translated by Katherine Prescott Wormeley, Lamb Publishing Co., New York, 1912.

Carroll, Stuart, *Martyrs and Murderers: The Guise Family and the Making of Europe*, Oxford University Press, Oxford, 2009.

Chamberlin, E. R., *Marguerite of Navarre*, Dial Press, New York, 1974.

Chappell Lougee, Carolyn, *Facing the Revocation, Huguenot Families, Faith, and the King's Will*, University Press, New York, 2017.

Freer, Martha Walker, *Henry III, King of France and Poland: His Court and Times*, 3 vols., Dodd, Mead and Company, New York, 1888.

Héritier, Jean, *Catherine de' Medici*, translated by Charlotte Haldane, George Allen & Unwin Ltd., 1963.

Knecht, R. J. *Catherine de' Medici*. Longman, London and New York, 1999
—— *Renaissance Warrior and Patron: The Reign of Francis I*, Cambridge University Press, Cambridge, 1994.

Le Plastrier Webb, Denis, *The Le Plastrier and Allied Families*, Melbourne, 1984.

Machiavelli, Niccolò, *The Prince*, translated by George Bull, Penguin Classics, London, 2014.

Marguerite de Valois, *Memoirs of Marguerite de Valois, Queen of Navarre. Written by Herself*, Grolier Society, Paris and Boston, 1900.

Mme. Du Hausset, *Memoirs of Marguerite de Valois, Queen of France, Wife of Henri 1V; of Madame de Pompadour of the Court of Louis XV; and of Catherine de' Medici, Queen of France, Wife of Henri II*, P.F. Collier & Son, New York, 1910.

Pardoe, Miss [Julia] Harper, *Louis the Fourteenth, and the Court of France in the Seventeenth Century*, France, 1847.

Pernoud, Régine, *Joan of Arc: By Herself and Her Witnesses*, Lanham, MD, Scarborough House, 1982.

Pernoud, Régine, and Marie-Véronique Clin., *Joan of Arc: Her Story*, revised and translated by Jeremy DuQuesnay Adams, St. Martin's Griffin, New York, 1999.

Roeder, Ralph, *Catherine de' Medici and the Lost Revolution*, Viking Press, New York, 1937.

Roelker, Nancy Lyman, *Queen of Navarre: Jeanne d'Albret*, 1528 – 1572, The Belknap Press of Harvard University Press, Cambridge, Massachusetts, 1968.

Rosenfeld, Jason, *John Everett Millais*, Phaidon Press Ltd., London, 2012.

Sichel, Edith, *Catherine de' Medici and the French Reformation*, reprinted from the 1905 edition, University Press of the Pacific, Honolulu 2004 —— *The Later Years of Catherine de' Medici*, Archibald Constable & Co. Ltd., London, 1908.

Surtees, Robert Smith, *Jorrocks' Jaunts and Jollities*, reprinted from the 1843 edition, Serenity Publishers, Rockville, Maryland, 2010.

Vale, M. G. A., *Charles VII [French Monarchs]*, Methuen Publishing Ltd., London, 1974.

Van Dyke, Paul, *Catherine de Médicis*, 2 vols., Charles Scribner's Sons, New York, 1922.

Whitehead, A. W., *Gaspard de Coligny: Admiral of France*, Methuen & Co., London, 1904.

Williams, Hugh, N., *Henry II, His Court and Times*, Charles Scribner's Sons, New York, 1910.

ILLUSTRATION CREDITS

The cover of my book is from a copy of a painting by John Everett Millais, *A Huguenot, on St. Bartholomew's Day, Refusing to Shield Himself from Danger by Wearing the Roman Catholic Badge*. Oil on canvas, arched top, 92.7 x 62.2 cm, Makins Collection. Picture attributed to Alamy Images.

The Huguenot Monument – Photograph taken in 2017. Attributed to Helge Herrmann.

Catherine de Médicis. Attributed to Wikipedia [in the public domain].

St Bartholomew's Day Massacre. Attributed to Alamy Images.

Le Gros Horloge, and archway leading through to the Le Plastrier house, 23 rue du Gros Horloge – photograph taken in 2018. Attributed to Robert Schaerer.

Original road sign – photograph taken in 2018. Attributed to Robert Schaerer.

A drawing of 23 rue du Gros Horloge, the ancestral home of the Le Plastriers, bought by Jean Le Plastrier in 1662. Attributed to Denis Le Plastrier Webb, *The Le Plastrier and Allied Families*, 1984.

A similar 17th century house to the Le Plastriers' home in rue du Gros Horloge, showing the rear of the property. Attributed to Denis Le Plastrier Webb, *The Le Plastrier and Allied Families*, 1984.

The upper part of 23 rue du Gros Horloge [middle building in green]. Photo taken in 1984. Attributed to Denis Le Plastrier Webb, *The Le Plastrier and Allied Families*, 1984.

The Quevilly Temple, Rouen 1660. Attributed to Denis Le Plastrier Webb, *The Le Plastrier and Allied Families*, 1984.

Snargate Street, Dover. Attributed to Wikipedia [in the public domain].

ACKNOWLEDGEMENTS

A special thank you to Robert for not only helping to edit my manuscript, but for his advice and encouragement, without which I would never have written this book. To Laurian for her continued invaluable help and advice. To Terry for checking my French, and last but certainly not least to those of my friends who kindly took the time to so carefully proofread my manuscript.

ALSO BY ANTHEA RAMSAY

The Forgotten Pioneer

Kindle edition

Avaliable from online book shops

 Matador

For exclusive discounts on Matador titles,
sign up to our occasional newsletter at
troubador.co.uk/bookshop

CPSIA information can be obtained
at www.ICGtesting.com
Printed in the USA
BVHW051524290623
666557BV00004B/558